ACCIDENTS

DON'T

HAPPEN

Christina Sadler

Produced by *Blaisdon Publishing*
3 Park Chase, Hornby, Bedale,
North Yorkshire DL8 1PR
www.blaisdon.f9.co.uk

This Autobiography relates to actual events and
nothing is intended to vitiate, or misrepresent any
real persons, alive or dead.

Printed in Malta through Printworks Int. Ltd.

ISBN 1 902838 05 X

For

My finest teachers,

Tony and Laura Sadler,

With love.

Acknowledgements

My love and deep appreciation goes to my brother, David, for his patience, expert technical support and wonderful family, Kim, Becky, Jess and James.

Dr John Hargrave MBE for reconstructing my arm (and my mind).

Nicky for all her work and encouragement

Kathleen for her believing in the dream

Barbara for her meticulous attention to detail

Sue, Joanie, Dawn and Lyn for their boundless enthusiasm and laughter.

FH for being there.

Rob Compton CFII for teaching me to fly.

And finally, Leslie Parrish and Richard Bach
For proving that miracles can happen.

Christina

INTRODUCTION

Ireland 1963

It is a sunny day. Childhood memories seem to be bathed in that translucent light, showing that 'all is well'. There is concrete. A lot of concrete and some sort of a brick wall. I see four, five pairs of raised eyes, wide and awe-struck, looking up towards a small girl, perched on the end of that wall. Arms outstretched, chin cocked, facing the sky.

"Of course – You know I can fly."

A split second passed. They held their breath. Blind faith shining from their eyes. Then, the spell is broken by a loud rap on the kitchen window. Half-stern, half-bemused eyes could be seen through that window.

"Tina!"

The tiny girl's eyes cloud over with embarrassment and indignation as she humbly descends from her launch.

ONE

Australia. August 1987

This half memory kept haunting me, lying on the road. My body warm and sticky with blood, flowing slower now from the ragged end of my left arm. A mass of sinuous red flesh still twitched and jerked as if it had a life of its own. I clenched my teeth and moaned. My side was warm and wet. The outside world was losing its clarity, as my senses dulled and my mind withdrew.

Life is an obstacle race, I thought. Just when I felt I'd cleared the hardest obstacles and was racing ahead, fate had intervened by sticking out his hairy little leg and tripping me. I crashed to the ground feeling, oh, so cheated. The idea that my life was now coming to an abrupt end at so tender an age was more of a blow than the tree that had hurtled its way through the car to wrench off my left arm.

I wasn't easily surprised these days – but this! This was mind blowing. Like most twenty seven-year-olds, I'd thought I was pretty much invincible. There's plenty of time. Life goes on forever...

What had brought me here? What sort of events had steered me here to this particular outcome? I tried to move but as soon as I did a sharp pain ricocheted around inside my head. A frightened inner voice had taken over from my wailing.

" *Where – is – my – father?* "

He'd died a year ago.

Then a calmer more reasonable voice coaxed, *"Just close your eyes and drift off... you don't want to be here, really, do you? Together we can leave this horror."*

Why was I here, lying on a crumbled old track that looked as if it was used maybe once or twice a year, a hundred miles south of Darwin in the middle of the Australian outback?

"You've really done it this time," the voice went on.

I felt a pang of guilt sweep across my battered body, but I could weep no more. If I hadn't had this yearning for adventure I might still be safe in the bosom of my family in Yorkshire. Why was I like this? Was I searching or running? One would never know, and, although the blood coming out the end of my stump had now quelled to a slow dribble, I knew there wasn't a lot of time left to work it all out. Not that it mattered now. The words ' *if only...* ' kept coming into my clouded mind – *'If only I'd done this... if only I'd done that...'*

The sheer absurdity of my position hit me. I had wanted to do such a vast array of things. Was this some kind of punishment? The shock, that it would not now be possible, hit me with the impact of a sharp blow to the stomach. This turn of events had caught me completely by surprise. There had been no warning, no clues...or had there?

TWO

My mind scanned through the events that had brought me to this point in my life. Suddenly, I was looking back at a fresh-faced seventeen year-old. A long titian mane streamed out from beneath the bottle-green school bonnet.

"I'm definitely not going to get married until I'm at least twenty-five," she had announced to her friend on the way to school.

"No...neither am I!" replied the equally innocent schoolgirl at her side.

"There are so many things I need to do first," I continued.

"Yes, there are...what *do* we need to do first?"

"I'm not sure...but we will know when the time comes."

"Yes. We will know."

Helen had married two years later and was now firmly ensconced in a neat semi with two children. And here was she, Tina. The one who just one month ago had blithely said to the same friend over coffee,

"I don't feel any different to when I was seventeen!"

She didn't. That was the whole problem. Nothing in her life had changed. Everyone else's lives had moved on and here she was – the same. Where were the fireworks in her life? The momentous tasks she would have to perform? Yes, she had become a teacher – but, was that it?

Her life had begun to stagnate.

* * *

ENGLAND MAY 1987

I was standing at the window, trying to clear an area of condensation with the net curtain, so I could see out. The net curtain didn't help much, but I used it anyway, clearing an area large enough to see through the condensation on the inside of the living room window. A sad picture met my eyes. It was a damp and cloudy February day. Barely even a wisp of wind to stir one's interest in the scene outside. *Where was she?* I couldn't relax or sit down. I just paced up and down the lounge in exasperation. I don't know why I always get like this. The course was not due to start until the afternoon. I think it was just that I was ready and I hate wasting time. Finally, a pair of headlights swung into the drive and Gill shot out of a small car and scuttled down the drive towards my front door.

"Don't worry, Gill. We're going to have to kill some time before the course starts anyway," I blurted out, trying to calm her, "I'm ready now, so let's set off and stop somewhere for a coffee or something on the way down to Grantley Hall."

As we left my quaint hometown of Northallerton, Yorkshire, behind us, the sky ahead seemed brighter. Before long, the rain had stopped and bright sunshine lit the way, bathing our faces in warmth. Before we knew it, we were passing the turn off for Knaresborough. I'd once had a wonderful romance in that town during my first teaching practice. It stirred up warm feelings, as I saw the name of the town and pondered what might have been.

Below the main sign, there was a second one. A small sign in brown with the words *'Mother Shipton's Cave'* inscribed upon its surface and an arrow pointing in the direction of

Knaresborough. I looked at it then looked back at the road ahead.

"I've often wondered what that place is like." said Gill.

"What place is that?" I asked.

"Mother Shipton's Cave," she replied, "...it's somewhere you always mean to visit, but never actually get around to doing it."

"Can't say I've spared it much thought," I answered, then, trying to feign interest, "What's there?"

"Well, it's Mother Shipton's Cave. There's a petrifying well and something else, I think it's a wishing well. Legend has it that Mother Shipton was England's most famous Prophetess. She lived some five hundred years ago."

Gill was into all these mystical things in a big way.

"Well...we've got time...if you want to see it...why not go now?" I surprised myself by saying.

We pulled off the road at the next turn off and doubled back. It wasn't long before we picked up the signs for the cave.

"This is so exciting," she grinned, "I love stuff like this."

Unbelievably, the sun was glistening over the river by the time we parked the car and I walked into the little house to buy our entrance tickets. The whole place was deserted, except, that is, for an old couple sharing a pot of tea and a scone. This place was not your usual hi-tech tourist trap. No flashing lights or fluorescent colours. No tacky toys. The walls were simply whitewashed. The floor was wooden and in the tiny windows hung tired old net curtains that had definitely seen better days. There was an old scroll pinned up on one of the walls. Gill ran over to it.

"Just listen to this...

     'Carriages without horse shall go, and accidents fill the world with woe.
Around the world thoughts shall fly
In the twinkling of an eye.
Iron in the water shall float
As easy as a wooden boat
Gold shall be found and found in
A land that's not known.'

"This is mind-blowing," whispered Gill, "all this was written five hundred years ago, come on let's look around."

On stepping outside, we saw a sign pointing down in the direction of the River Nidd. Even though it was still winter, the classical landscaped carriage drive through the ancient forest of Knaresborough was beautiful. Tall beech trees stretched themselves in the sun.

First, we came to the petrifying well. Various objects had been turned to stone. It was fun discovering all the weird objects that had been hung there over the years, being petrified by the dripping water in the cave. Children would say it was magic. More worldly adults can explain it away – but why do people always feel they have to? This place certainly had a certain strange feel to it – or was it just my imagination?

Next, we stumbled along the muddy track to the wishing well. It was so peaceful here. The water, wind, everything seemed to stand still.

"Look, here it is," Gill shouted back from around the corner.

"All our troubles end here, Tina, look...it says you just have to place your left hand into the water, and make your wish and let the water dry on your hand. Easy as that!" she laughed.

I closed my eyes and slowly plunged my left hand deep into the murky waters of the well.

"Don't tell me what you're wishing for – just think it."

I scrunched up my eyes and wished as hard as I could for money. Strange thing to wish for really, but I did. I wished for wealth. My reasoning was that money would free me to discover my 'true' path.

The task complete, I opened my eyes and shook the water from my freezing left hand. The spell was placed. The die was cast...

THREE

I still don't know where to start when talking about my father. I try to think about him and some distant door slams shut and that old familiar constriction starts to creep around my throat. I always lived in fear of losing him.

I remember once...we were living in Germany. I must have been no more than seven or eight years old...waking up howling,

"...Please don't die... please don't die!"

He hadn't had much of a childhood to speak of, so, at the tender age of fourteen he decided enough was enough and proceeded to join the British Army as a boy soldier. It was during this time that he became a boxer and fought his way to becoming Army Boxing Association Welter-weight champion of England – something that he never thought to mention. I happened to find out whilst we were out walking along the sea front at Saltburn. A stranger stopped in front of us and stared at him saying,

"Excuse me, aren't you Tony Sadler, the boxer?"

I started to giggle but this person went on,

"...I watched you fight in The Royal Albert Hall in London."

You see, by the time I came along, my father was the only person left in his family. He had long since lost touch with his mother and half-brother. There was nobody left to tell me anything about him other than himself, and he didn't do things like that. So, he remains to this day something of an enigma.

He was a Red Beret in the Parachute Regiment when he met my mother. She was a Barbara Stanwyck look-a-like, with her chestnut mane sweeping over her crisp, white peasant blouse tucked into her dirndl skirt.

She was on the floor dancing at Queen's Hall in Farnborough when he first spied her. Shortly after my father's arrival, her partner left the floor and was mysteriously never heard from again...my father stepped in and their destinies became intertwined.

When he met my mother, he finally found true love. She became his world. Several years after their marriage, David and I were born and his world was now complete. He had never had a family of his own My mother, too, although she had experienced a far happier childhood, had been raised without a father. Neither one of them had known what it was like to be part of a normal family unit.

He was devoted to us. We were the first family that he had ever really known. Everything lacking in his own childhood he poured into ours. It was a magical time filled with fantasy, mystery and, of course, fairies. When he was in the Army, he would be sent away quite often on training exercises. Although I hated his leaving, I loved the letters he would send me. Stories of leprechauns and 'the little people'...complete with illustrations. He wrote me funny, rhyming poems and always called me 'Red' because of my hair. When he was sent to Cyprus for six months, he read all the '*Borrowers*' stories on to tape and sent them to me so that I would not have to go to bed without my bedtime story. He always felt that fantasy should be encouraged in children, and squirmed when he witnessed parents trying to rob their offspring of their childhood by allowing them to access the adult world too soon.

Each evening after work, he would take me back down to his gym. It always seemed to smell of sweaty socks and leather 'medicine balls'. I felt both grand and important that he should unlock the doors to the Regimental gym just for his little girl. Once inside, he would give me lessons in gymnastics and trampolining. At the time, I took all of this for granted and thought every daddy spent this much time with his children.

Receiving my first set of gardening tools, I recall having to bury an old cauliflower in the earth. I was told to wait and see what happened overnight. Sure enough, the next day, the fairies *had* been busy. Hardly able to contain myself, using my bare hands, I dug down deep in the ground, the rich, moist Irish soil flying in all directions, to find out what had happened to my mouldy old cauliflower. Suddenly, my hands touched something hard. Pushing away the earth, a bright and gleaming set of implements was revealed. The fairies had smiled down on the little girl on that day.

He nurtured and protected us (maybe a little too much) and filled our lives with wonderment, charm and delight. He adored children and was in his element when he was with them. A few weeks before Christmas each year, I would write a letter to Saint Nicholas in Greenland. This was a major affair. I would tell him all my news, asking how he was and how the reindeer were doing – and then slip in somewhere that I would really, really love a *Barbie Doll* for Christmas!

I could hardly contain the excitement I felt, as I stood on my tiptoes to mail the letter on its way to Greenland.

Then, one day, I was about seven or eight, I returned from school in a distraught state. I ran into the living room in floods of tears.

"Mum, Dad..." I cried, "Alan Gooding says there's no such thing as Father Christmas...is it true?...it's not true, is it?"

My parents glanced across to one another and then my father took me by the hand and led me to a chair.

"You see, Teen...it's like magic really...if enough children in the world believe in Father Christmas...then he will exist. If they believe that he does really fly around the world bringing happiness to all the little children...then he will. It is only by believing in something that it becomes real. If everyone stops believing...he will no longer exist."

When my mother reminded me of this episode, during the writing of this book, I was astounded by the profundity of his explanation. Needless to say, I kept up my letter writing to the North Pole for some time after that.

My Mum was usually the more grounded of the two. She was the perfect foil to my father's whimsical character. She would play along. Then, when the time came she would bring us back down to reality. When times were tough financially, my mother would scrape together just enough money during the week for us to have a decent Sunday dinner. Then my Dad would roll up brandishing a bottle of pink champagne to wash it down!

* * *

I was born October 3rd 1959 in the British Military Hospital in Rinteln, West Germany. My father was by now a respected Physical Training Instructor, attached to the Ninth/Twelfth Lancers. He was in charge of the physical training of the Regiment.

One of his tasks was to coach the regimental soccer team and it was as my mother was standing on the doorstep of their army quarter in Detmold, waving off the bus that transported this team to a local fixture that I started to make my entrance to this world. The bus screeched to a halt and she was unceremoniously bundled into the back and rushed along the tiny winding roads to the hospital. She was dumped there and my father went off to his match. She later told me that it was not considered 'proper' for fathers to be present at the birth in those days. So there she was, alone in a foreign country, miles away from home and family, about to give birth to her first child.

"That was the way it was...we didn't question everything... we just got on with it."

When the hospital staff heard that this was a first baby they relaxed, thinking that she was just over-reacting. She was placed on a bed in a room and left alone, despite her repeatedly telling staff that I was on my way.

As my head began to show, my mother shouted to a cleaning lady to go and get help, but I had already catapulted myself into this world by the time anyone came. My mother maintains that I have been the same ever since – barging ahead, waiting for nothing and no one (I am not sure if this a fair comment). I was born with a mop of fiery red hair. My mother had long, wavy chestnut hair and my father, jet-black curls.

The soccer team won their match that morning and so insisted that the coach's baby daughter be present at each and every match played from then on, shivering in a push-chair on the sidelines.

We moved all around Germany, Scotland and Northern Ireland, never staying in one place for much more than a year. Each time we changed Regiments, I had to leave one set of friends and seek new ones. Gradually, I began to get the feeling of not belonging anywhere. I didn't seem to be part of anything permanent. My direct family was the only constant in my life.

Summer vacations were the highlight of my childhood. Each year, my father would save up all the canned food issued to soldiers during training exercises. The moment there was enough to fill the trunk of our *Fiat 125*, he would sling us all in the car, along with a couple of tents and go AWOL (absent without leave). He drove non-stop to the shores of Lake Garda, Italy, and there we would stay, catching fish and living off that revolting army food. But we were in heaven.

The campsite there was extremely basic. A piece of land too rough to be called arable, it could have supported a few olive trees I expect. But, after Marta and Eva had erected a ramshackle sanitation-hut, café and shop on the field and planted a few trees to shade the little tents from the harsh mid-day sun, they had themselves the perfect campsite. And people came from all over the world to stay at '*Camping La Foche*', nestled along the shores of Largo Di Garda, between the towns of Toscolano and Moderno.

I spent my first summer there at eighteen months. Red hair is not prevalent amongst the Italians. They told me when I was a little girl that people with red hair are thought to be angels come down from heaven. Wherever I went, amply bosomed Italian mamas would scoop me up into their arms exclaiming, "...ahhhh...bambina rossa!" I revelled in all the attention from these exuberant females.

My brother and I learnt to swim in those crystal clear waters – so pure because they were formed from the melted snow from the Alps. I played with kids from all over the world. We didn't speak each other's languages, but that didn't stop us communicating. I loved to find out about their countries and customs. Even life in the army quarters was an education for me. At one point, we were placed near an old gypsy encampment. Gypsies were not allowed to roam around the countryside in Germany, so I was able to befriend this delightful free spirit in the form of Silvana – a Romany child a year or two my senior. We revelled in each other's company. Again unable to speak a word of the other's tongue, we had no problem communicating. It wasn't long until I was wrenched away from her, too.

Languages were never a big problem, since I spent my early years in the company of children from all around the world. I ended up being able to converse not only in several tongues, but could also change my accent like a chameleon to suit all occasions and allow maximum acceptance. This was not because I had any special linguistic ability; I put it down to the fact that I am an inquisitive person by nature. I love finding out about other people and I was hardly going to let a foreign language or accent impede this process. I also craved acceptance. So one could hear me move from a clipped 'Queen's English' accent to a Scottish brogue to a broad Yorkshire accent depending on which crowd I was with at the time. I catch myself doing it even to this day.

Apart from one brief stay in England when my brother was born, we didn't move back until I was ten years old. I had spent most of my formative years in Germany and had formed a strong affinity with that country. England didn't feel like my country, somehow. When we returned to England, I bawled for the entire flight back in that old *Dakota* aircraft.

I suppose that if my Father had a fault, it was that we grew up believing that the world was full of kind and loving people who would never dream of hurting us. The harsh reality seemed to triple in intensity when, some years later, we did go out into the real world and found it wasn't quite as we had expected!

I was twenty-three and had been dating this man for a long time. We had chosen the wallpaper and decorated together. I was deliriously happy. Then one bright and shining morning in May I decided that, since Roy was at work, I would go around and paint a window frame that needed doing. As I walked into the house, I immediately noticed that the curtains in the living-room had not been opened. Thinking he was sick, I ran up stairs and found him in bed. He was not alone. My whole world crumbled before my eyes. It was a harsh introduction to the real world and shook me to the very foundations. At the time, I truly felt that this was the worst thing that could happen to anyone. Little did I know.

In the meantime, my father had been suffering from intestinal problems. Religiously, he went to the doctor and was told to drink peppermint tea to settle his stomach. He once went and told the doctor that the only way he could digest a meal was to drink half a bottle of *Milk of Magnesia*. The doctor advised him to continue drinking his peppermint tea. My father never burdened us with these problems until it was too late. Finally, whatever was causing the problem grew so large that it blocked the intestine completely. They could no longer tell him to go away and drink tea. He was taken straight into hospital and the blockage was removed. He was very sick following the operation, but we were relieved it was over.

I was applying for a new job at the time and had been so badly affected by my father's condition that I didn't think that I would be able to withstand the strain involved in going through a rigorous interview. As soon as it was morning break at school, I jumped into the car and sped off to seek the advice of my father in hospital; I wanted to know his thoughts on the matter (although I secretly knew what his answer would be). On arriving, I noticed that my father's Consultant was at his bedside, so I lingered outside the ward in the corridor. After a few minutes as the Consultant made to exit the ward, I stood up in front of him and told him that I was Mr Sadler's daughter and wanted to know how he was progressing. The man looked uncomfortable and said that my father was still recovering from a very serious operation. I should have just accepted this but, being the person I am, I asked the question which would change my life from that time forth. I asked when the biopsy results from the tumour were due back. We were praying they would verify that it had been a non-malignant tumour.

Still in the corridor - people were wandering back and forth past us as he said, "There's no need to wait for them...it was obvious from the start that it was a very large, malignant tumour causing the blockage."

My whole body went numb. The only way I was able to hang on to the present was by fixing my eyes firmly on his. I was being held upright by forcing myself to stare into his eyes. People were still bustling past.

I said, "Well...did you get it all out?"

"We got the tumour out, but there are secondaries...on the liver."

Ice-cold despair surged through my veins. I didn't know much about cancer, but I did know that the liver was bad news.

"How-how long do you give him?"

"Six to nine months...but there's one thing I must insist upon...he is too sick to know about this at present...he must not know."

"What about my mother?"

I couldn't understand how my brain was still functioning and my mouth was still issuing words when I had just died inside.

"If you think she has the ability to hide something like this from someone she loves...tell her."

There was no way that she could do something like that. It would be like asking the sun to stop shining.

I walked away from that man and had about twenty seconds to get a grip on myself. He must not know. Taking a deep breath, I swung around the corner and watched my dad's eyes light up. I proceeded to discuss the job interview with him and got the swift answer I had expected.

'Go ahead with it. Never quit.'

Later, I had asked him whether he had the slightest inclination about what had taken place just before seeing him - in that busy corridor. He said that there had been no indication whatsoever that anything was wrong. And there was no one more astute than my father.

I returned to school and eventually, at the end of the worst day of my life, I left for home. On the way I sought the refuge of a neighbour – a kind-hearted lady who sat, listened and said very little. When I finally made it home, my mother had cooked a large chicken dinner. I took one look and knew there was no way it could pass my lips.

I realise now, that I must have been in shock, but then I thought it really bizarre. Anyone who knows anything about me knows that food is my passion. As soon as my mother left the room, I made straight for the drinks cabinet and pulled out a bottle of vodka (I loathe vodka). I drank a quarter of a bottle straight.

My mother had been sleeping in my spare bed in my room ever since Dad had entered hospital. When finally we made it to bed, I was exhausted but too frightened to sleep, lest I spoke about the day's events. So, I just stayed awake. I did this crazy thing day and night for three days. My mother was beginning to get suspicious. My behaviour was becoming alarming. I thought I was going insane. Then, on the fourth day, it suddenly dawned on me that I had no right to withhold such information from her. She was his wife.

I had to do it at a time that would allow her the most time to gather herself before facing my dad. Straight after a visit would be best. I went about it in a calm and systematic way. As soon as she left, I dimmed the living-room lights and made the room warm. Then I went into the kitchen and made a large pot of sweetened tea. I had heard somewhere that sweet tea was good for shock. Then I sat and waited.

The clock in the sitting room had just finished chiming nine o'clock when our back door swung open and my Mum stuck her head round the door. I looked at her and wondered how the hell I was going do what I now had to. She appeared to be quite bright and cheerful. My father still had the ability to cheer people up even under these circumstances.

"Your Father's looking a lot better, Teen...more like his old self. Looks like we might be able to go on that holiday with Hilda and Bill after all."

She looked so happy, I almost abandoned everything, but I knew she had to know this. It was her right to know the truth. I had no right to withhold this. So, I sat her down and told her everything. It was the hardest thing I have ever had to do. At first, she didn't want to believe my words, but then she knew she had no choice. I had expected her to either break down sobbing, or stick her chin out and put on a brave face. She did neither. She just sat there and shook uncontrollably. It sounds ludicrous, but in the end, we were laughing because she couldn't stop shaking and I kept trying to pour sweetened tea into her.

When the news was finally out in the open, my father insisted that my brother David finish his studies at college about three hundred miles away and would not allow him to come home and interrupt his education. Dave did as my Dad had decreed, but I knew his heart was breaking.

None of us were prepared for the speed of his deterioration. In a few short months, we watched helplessly as the proud, athletic, muscular man we knew turned into a dignified but dithery ninety year old, unable to shave himself. We were all in limbo trying to pretend it wasn't happening, but unable to halt the fast forward button on our dad's precious life. We hated to see him lose his dignity, but, of more consequence, was the fact that he hated *us* to see him like this. He hated to see our pain. He had spent his life protecting us all from this kind of thing and here he was causing it. He refused his painkilling pills in the end, because he said they were interfering with his conscious mind. He needed to remain lucid, because he wanted to write a story for my mother. He had written several short stories during his latter years and had always promised my mother that she would get one. He was trying to read it onto tape. He started it too late – it never got finished.

It was one o'clock in the morning when the phone rang. We had been warned he might not make it through the night. When it rang we all knew why. An anger in me finally exploded. For a split second, the world stopped and a wrath erupted from the epicentre of my consciousness. I swung round and vented my frustration by smacking my foot into an enormous cushion in front of me. It flew across the room.

"No!" I roared and then made for the door, trying despe-

rately to gain control of myself.

Nobody had heeded my pleas. I had begged the Universe to spare him and had been ignored. What was the point of his being taken from us now? He was doing such tremendous work with the glue-sniffing, drug-taking gangs in Middlesbrough, Britain's worst employment black spot. He made a difference in everyone's lives he touched. All the kids he worked with adored him. Perhaps because they knew he had 'been there'.

We filed out of the house to the car. This wasn't happening. On the way to the hospital, we passed a drunk staggering up the street. I saw red,

"Why the bloody hell does he have the right to live when my father is dying?"

I had never spoken like that before, especially not in front of my mother, but nothing was said. We gathered round his bed and, right up to the end, I was trying to force him to drink some water. Then, without warning, he sat bolt upright and smiled, staring straight ahead. His wonderful mop of black curls now faded and grey. His vibrant rich brown eyes were strained and washed out, but for those last few seconds I saw a whisper of his former glory. A nurse came in and told us that he would die within the next five minutes and if we didn't want to witness it, we were to leave.

I couldn't watch him die. I wanted only to remember him alive. I left and the door slammed behind me. Now I was on my own. Mum stayed with him, holding his hand. Devoid of emotion, I lent up against the shiny primrose painted wall and closed my eyes. I suppose that, even then, I still thought it wasn't real and that I would wake up only to find it was a dreadful nightmare.

Suddenly every ounce of energy left my body. My

legs buckled and I slid down the wall, ending up in a heap on the floor.   At that precise moment, Mum came out and announced that he had gone.   We stared at each other, but neither of us could speak.   Then, on cue, there came the loudest crack of thunder followed by several others.   The rain came pounding down and there was a power outage throughout the hospital.   Lightning splashed across the sky. For a brief moment, Mum and I cut through each other's pain and smiled.   At least he had gone out with a bang!

"Come on," she cried, "...we must call Dave."

The church was brimming over with tattooed, spiky-haired youths with tear stained faces.   One particularly hard-faced lad turned to his neighbour saying,

"I never knew the meaning of love until I met that man..."

Three Royal Air Force *Tornado* planes flew over the little graveyard just as we were lowering the coffin into the grave.

I glanced over, yet again, towards my mother.   Numb as we were with grief, an unspoken message passed between us.

'*This*... was no accident.'

FOUR

A morning in June. Sun filtering through the thin curtains in my room, filling it with that precious golden brightness, permeating even the deepest of slumbers. It was a mild morning – that cold, sharpness of winter had finally been overcome by spring. You could smell spring, feel it in your bones. The earth moves – it really does – as everything awakens and life begins once again. I stretched and filled my lungs with the morning air. It gave me a sense of well-being. Life wasn't so bad. I glanced over to the other side of my pretty little bedroom. I swung my legs round in the bed. As I pushed down to heave myself up, a searing pain shot up through my left arm and I immediately took the weight off it.

"What have you done, Teen?"

My mother rolled over, a look of befuddled consternation on her face.

"Oh, I don't know, I've done something to my arm," I said, "do you want a cup of coffee, I'm going down to make one?"

"Um, Yes please...but what's wrong with your hand?

"Oh, nothing. God Mum! If you haven't got anything to worry about, you invent stuff!"

Tripping over the lamp wire, almost pulling it off the night stand, perched precariously on three legs, next to my bed, I scrambled to the window, hesitating a moment before allowing the outside world to intrude upon mine. A cold grey mist added the final touch, perfecting the cold picture that met my eyes. I effortlessly trudged down the stairs to the kitchen. The uneasy silence one feels when walking into an empty cinema hung in this room, seeming to augment the gaping chasm left by the absence of my father. I switched on the reassuring voice of the DJ. I always listened to this part of the programme before setting off for work.

I was starting to make the coffee, when I was bothered once again by the bizarre pain in my wrist. I picked up the kettle and took it over to the tap to fill. As I grabbed the tap to turn it on, yet another searing pain shot up my arm. I was more annoyed than worried and tried to work out how I'd hurt my wrist. No, I couldn't remember doing anything to aggravate this condition.

I went to school. At that time, I taught children with learning disabilities. I was still suffering considerable discomfort in my left wrist. I sat there trying to lose myself in my teaching, but the throbbing persisted. By now, I was feeling pretty sick. The pupils could sense that something was amiss. I couldn't muster up the unusual energy needed to ignite the spark necessary to get through to young people who have become comfortable with failure. I turned on my heel and reached for a pile of exercise books behind me. On lifting the pile, suddenly my wrist gave way and an excruciating pain shot up my arm. The kids' eyes lit up with laughter as the pile of books flew into the air and scattered themselves all over the wooden floor of the classroom. One or two pupils shot forward,

"I'll get them. I'll get them for you Miss," I heard them shout as they pushed their way towards the offending books.

"Shall we give them out for you Miss?" asked Paul, a tiny boy with beautiful brown eyes and a wickedly hilarious sense of humour.

"Yes, thanks Paul," I mumbled, not so much embarrassed, as shaken by the apparent loss of strength in my left arm.

I just couldn't understand this. I don't like being unable to reason things out. This one had me baffled.

"Jacky, Can I have a quick word?" I whispered to our Deputy Head, later on that morning.

"Sure, come on in. What's the problem?"

Jacky Varty was the Medical Officer in the school, in charge of all First Aid training for both staff and pupils.

"It's my arm, well, my wrist actually...will you have a quick look at it...it's been throbbing all morning and, to tell you the truth, I'm feeling quite sick from it."

She glanced up sharply,

"What have you done to it?"

"Nothing, as far as I can remember – just woke up like this."

I was hoping she would produce a miracle pill and send me on my way with a reassuring word or two. She scrutinised my face, noticing the thin film of sweat coating my upper lip and the pallid colour around my eyes and cheeks.

"If you're feeling nauseous – that's the sign of a fracture. I suggest you pop down to the hospital and get an X-ray."

This is crazy, I thought as I drove my car out of the school and towards the hospital, cradling my pained arm in my lap. There's quite a knack to this one-handed driving! My car was not automatic.

"You'll be pleased to know, that nothing has shown up on the X-ray. You've probably just strained it or something. I'm going to put a splint on – to immobilise it for a while. That should do it."

The portly lady doctor finally looked up at me peering over her gold half-framed glasses – eye contact having finally been made for the first time, a good five minutes into the consultation. Driving home was even more of a problem now that the wrist was totally inflexible, but I was getting used to one-armed driving by now.

Time went on. I had tried to use the arm a couple of times, but I just met with disaster. I found I couldn't even lift a cup of tea or a plate with it. Weeks passed and I gradually learned how to dress and cook and wash and drive without using it. It became second nature to drive my car using just the right arm. Every now and then I would test out the left hand – but as soon as I did – a sharp pain shot up and immobilised it. It had been a month now, and I was starting to feel slightly anxious about the lack of improvement.

I had long since planned a holiday, a long holiday round the world. It was something I had needed for a long time now: an escape. All the plans were going smoothly. The ticket was booked. The insurance purchased. It was a way, I suppose, of buying myself some time to grieve over my father's death. Yes, everything was going like clockwork – all, that is, except one niggling little problem – the wrist was no better at all. It had been immobilised for well over a month. I wasn't concerned about the wrist itself. It was more the thought of how I would manage all my luggage with only one arm functioning as it should.

As a last resort, I decided to go to an osteopath. Perhaps they would be able to locate the offending bone and manipulate it back into place. Problem solved. So, along to the osteopath I trotted, feeling very optimistic. Why hadn't I thought of this before? I was led into a very clinically decorated room and told to wait. Mrs. Thompson would be with me in a few minutes.

"What can I help you with?"

A rather austere looking lady in her mid-forties lowered herself into the chair beside me, gracefully smoothing out the creases in her starched uniform.

"I've had a pain in my wrist for over a month now..."

As she listened, she took hold of my arm and began to press various areas around the bony part of the lower fore arm. I concluded my tale of woe and she put my arm back on the couch placing hers back in her lap. Looking directly at me, she took a deep breath and sighed.

"What's the matter?" I asked.

"I'm sorry Madam, but I'm not going to do anything to that wrist."

"Not going to do anything? What are you talking about? You haven't even tried yet?"

"I'm very sorry, but that wrist feels very strange to me. I'm not going to risk any kind of manipulation."

"Feels strange! What do you mean? Surely there is something you can do?"

"I suggest you go and get another X-ray. It feels very strange to me."

This arm was starting to really annoy me now. It made no sense to me that it was not improving. I returned to the doctor and persuaded him to send me for yet another X-ray.

I was surprised when the same portly little lady doctor that had treated me on my first visit entered my cubicle.

"Mm! This is the second X-ray. Still no better? I think I'll send this one away. It may be that one of the tiny bones is fractured or something – your X-ray needs greater magnification...it will be a few weeks before we get the results back."

'Oh well, that's it then...no more time left.' I thought privately.

I was due to leave for Singapore the following week. I now had to resign myself to the fact that nothing would be sorted out before my departure. Everything happens for a reason...I wonder what the reason for this could be.

FIVE

Australia

The sound of a mournful wail jolted me momentarily back to the present. It had issued from my own mouth. I'd had my eyes firmly closed for some time now, not wishing to be assaulted once again, by the sight of spiky bone surrounded by white, frilly flesh.

We had been driving along the dirt track road, heading for the Kakadu Nature Reserve in the Northern Territory. I believe there had been some heavy rain. The dirt road had been turned to mush and a truck or something had evidently made its way along it. The truck had left deep tracks along the road that, in turn, had baked hard as soon as the merciless Australian sun had hit the earth.

We had been driving steadily along this road, when our tyres slipped inadvertently into these old tracks. It felt as if we were on a rail track – there was no response to the steering wheel. Margot automatically attempted to pull the car out of these tracks, but first attempts proved futile. Somehow, in what seemed liked the next instance, we had left the dirt track completely and were bouncing, out of control, down a ravine. It was Margot's new car, a *Holden*, and had it not been for my visit to Australia, we would not have been in this predicament now.

There must have been a moment of impact, because whenever I hear that dull, deep, metal crunching thud following several minutes of screeching tyres in action-packed movies, I always feel nauseous. We didn't panic. It all happened so quickly. I don't know if I lost consciousness for a while. I do remember that the car finally settled into a hissing smoky heap on the hard, red earth. I had pain. I tried to breathe, but found I could not. Pain wracked my whole body, but nothing to forewarn me that anything serious had happened. I remember looking around through the smoke and dust. Everything seemed to be happening in slow motion.

"Get-out-of-the-car-now!" shrieked my friend.

She may have been worried that the car was about to explode. My brain had not yet got into gear. I was still sitting there quite happily, watching everything as if I were not part of the action.

I recall moving my arm up to open the car door, still unaware that anything was wrong. I swung it around, it moved much faster and quicker than a normal length arm. Consequently, I almost hit myself in the face with this bleeding, jerking stump.

I had no inkling of the loss of my limb, until I actually saw it. But that had been about two hours ago now – before I'd closed out reality.

"Oh, my God! This is a nightmare."

Then blackness. I could hear things, but see nothing. All the light had gone from my world. I found myself imagining the sound of a car and the slamming of a car door. It was wishful thinking.

I was weak now. The sun beat down and I could now hear insects buzzing around my bleeding stump. Was I still alive? I began to wonder. I withdrew away from the horror a little more, but I could still hear what was going on. Then I saw smoke or clouds whirling and moving – forming themselves into a long tunnel. I felt myself being pulled toward that tunnel. I wanted to go. I *really* wanted to go. I can still remember the happiness when I saw it – but after a while, I became aware of a little voice. It sounded like that of a small girl pleading.

"...*but I haven't finished yet – I haven't finished yet.*"

It was probably the voice of my conscience. It must have had quite some power – because I really did want to go. The whole incident meant nothing to me at the time. I put it down to the fact that I had been hallucinating, but it was something I was never to forget. Two or three years later, I walked into our lounge and there on the television was an exact image of my tunnel.

"Wha-what's this?" I asked my mother

"Oh, its just one of those programmes on Near-Death Experiences..." she answered.

A shiver wound its way up my spine...

***

A car door slammed.

Another car door slammed.

"Are you okay? Oh, my God. Where's all that blood coming from?"

My senses flooded back. This time it was real. I could hear a voice. My mind was confused. I wasn't as happy as I should have been at the sound of humanity. I had got myself into a state that felt quite comfortable – like a nice warm bed on a Sunday morning. This intrusion would mean I would have to get up.

"Shut up!" someone screamed. "She's lost her arm. I don't know what other injuries she's got...she won't let us near her."

Somebody mentioned something about medication and would it help at all. Then, blackness again. After sometime – I don't know how long – I felt someone holding my right hand. It was a leathery, strong hand.

"Hang on, girl!" a voice comforted me from above.

The flimsy cloth covering my stump was removed. I lurched expecting pain, but there was none. Only the drone of those hungry sand flies still darting around it.

"I'm going to tie this neckerchief around your arm. It won't hurt," said the voice of a man, so gentle yet so powerful, I couldn't have prevented him from helping me, even if I'd wanted to.

I turned my head towards the voice and forced open one eyelid. At first, the sheer glare of the sun blinded me. I blinked several times. Then tried to focus on the dark image between the sun and myself, which merely silhouetted his body, enhancing the mystique of this being. I knew, instinctively, that he was aboriginal, even before the glossy, corkscrew curls, forming a halo around his dark image, became apparent.

"We move you now to the truck." said the voice.

"Where's my arm? I want my arm," I croaked in a low whisper.

"What she say?"

He looked towards Pauline.

"She wants her arm to go with her," replied a dazed old friend.

"Where de arm?"

"I don't know"

Metal, glass and debris littered the area around the car. He took hold of my right arm. Pauline told me later that he looked over towards one of his Countrymen, a bewildered fellow of considerably less stature, dressed in a shabby vest and an over generous pair of frayed jeans, and bellowed, "You! Go find dat arm!" pointing with his lips in the direction of the Bush.

The smaller man's eyes had widened as he looked behind himself and, on seeing nobody, realised that Harry was talking to him. He swallowed hard and said,

"Who? *Me*?"

"Yes, you...go find dat arm."

It was found a few minutes later and was laid to rest in a ice-box filled with rapidly melting ice, taking the place of a rather nice little Riesling – meant for happier times. One person took hold of me under the arms and someone else my legs. I was lifted, so very gently, into a truck. I started to feel some discomfort. The road was so bumpy, and I felt as if my whole body was shattered and all the broken edges were clanging together with every jolt.

I must have lost consciousness then, because I remember coming to and being hit quite hard around the face.

After some time, the old truck pulled into Belyuen. I opened my eyes enough to see the face of an Aboriginal girl racing alongside the truck. I was already familiar with several people here, because I had visited the school the day before, during their annual Sports Day. The last thing I wanted was these children to be exposed to the sight of my partially dismembered body.

"Get those kids away from this truck... now."

The next part is vague. A green wooden hut. There were strong smells; musty smells mingled with the smell of my blood. Muslin curtains. A panic-stricken aboriginal 'medical officer', qualified only to administer *Aspirin* and *Band Aids*.

The Headmaster of the school came running in.

"I've radioed for the Flying Doctor Service in Broken Hill – reckons he'll be here in about an hour."

It had now been almost three and a half hours since the accident.

"Call my family – tell my family."

I thought I was dying.

I lay there and lay there in my twilight zone, feeling so weak I couldn't think any more.

Meeting the Aboriginal children at their school Sports Day

(Day before my accident)

SIX

Australia

"What did you say her name was? Tina? Okay – Tina! Tina! Can you hear me? Tina – Tina. I am Doctor Allen. I am going to put an IV into you. Can you hear me? You're going to feel a small jab."

Hear him? Of course, I could hear him. I could hear everything. I just felt like an objective observer of the situation. I was fully aware of what was happening, but it was as if it was happening to someone else and I didn't feel the need to participate in the situation.

"Sleep," I whispered, "just give me something to sleep."

Heartened that he'd finally elicited a response – he continued, "You've lost a lot of blood Tina. We need to get some fluid into you first…okay – then we'll see about everything else – good girl, you're doing well."

I drifted off – trying to smile.

'Everything's going to be okay now.'

Hours seemed to pass, but there still seemed to be no signs of my getting to a hospital, or even to a plane. The one little jab he told me about had now turned into several, not only in my arm but also in my feet and my ankles.

"Get me to a hospital," I urged, mustering up the energy to raise one eyelid enough to peer through the lashes at the doctor.

He was looking worried.

"Her veins have collapsed," I heard him say, "I can't find

one that can accept a needle."

'Oh Jesus! An incompetent doctor,' I thought, 'just what I need at this precise moment in time!'

I exhaled slowly, not feeling any kind of panic now, just slightly blurred and fuzzy. Light-headed. The sensation wasn't unpleasant. Everything just continues happening around you, but in slow motion. You see disturbing things happening, but nothing seems to matter anymore.

I wondered if this was what dying was like. No wonder my father had looked so serene when the nurse had come into his room to tell us he would die in five minutes and we were to decide if we wanted to be present or not. My poor father. Poor us. It seemed as if the very essence of our being had died with him on that stormy night in Yorkshire. God, even here in some remote part of Australia, with strangers flying around trying to get me to hospital – the memory of his death was still raw. I could hear the words of the vicar at his funeral.

"Tony was a man who lived his life to the full. He strove for perfection and I was not at all surprised to discover that his favourite book was Jonathan Livingston Seagull. He..."

These impressive but totally inadequate words floated away, as I tried to form my own idea of a man who was unquestionably my ultimate hero.

I was ten years old when my father's twenty two years in the army were up and we were thrown out in 'Civvy Street'. It was a big adjustment for all of us. Dad found himself back at college studying to be a social worker with a class full of eighteen-year-olds. I received a nasty jolt when I went to my first Civvy school and found that, instead of floating along effortlessly and coming out top of the class in every subject, I was no longer 'king pin'. For the first time in my life, I had to stretch myself just to keep up. Luckily, I had a teacher who saw that I did. I both disliked humiliation and feared her at the time, so I pulled out all the stops and passed the entrance exam to the local Grammar School.

By the time I had spent a couple of years there, I had discovered that the way to gain maximum acceptance was not by academic prowess, but in fact by the opposite. So, I took up the hem of my bottle green uniform so that it barely covered my behind and teetered around the school on platform shoes. Our gang would meet in the girls' toilets where we would share our cigarettes and have séances. Our favourite lesson was Physical Education. We would enthusiastically opt to do the cross-country run up Sandy Bank, but would veer off course long before that steep incline and find ourselves sipping coffee and smoking in someone's front room. This was fun! Then we traipsed down to the family planning clinic and got 'kitted out' with the pill. I suspect that the others, like me, had absolutely no use for it at that time, but it felt as if we were really grown up if we had it sitting in our dresser drawer

Then, one day, something hit the proverbial fan. I arrived home to find that my parents had been summoned to school to attend a meeting with my favourite teacher, Mr Trench. He had been watching my deteriorating behaviour and decided that it was time to step in. Not only that, my mother's *pièce de résistance* was that she dragged me up the stairs, flung open my dresser drawer and demanded to know what I was doing with the pills in my drawer. I protested my innocence, but the evidence to them looked pretty conclusive. I could not look at the pain I saw in my father's eyes. The shame it brought upon me that day with my parents was crippling. I responded angrily to their accusations and insinuations. I felt that my bubble had burst. I had to get away. I could go off to Europe and work as a travel courier. There was always a call for people with several languages.

I went to bed that night determined to find such a job the very next day. I had failed my parents and could see no alternative. My head throbbed as I buried it in my pillow. I sobbed and sobbed and finally fell into a deep sleep. Some hours later, I became aware that there was something in my room. I remember sensing this even before I awoke. I was curled up facing the wall, but knew that whatever it was had appeared behind me in the corner of my room diagonally opposite. When I finally summoned the courage to turn around, still knowing that there would be something there, I saw a figure appear. It was fluorescent. The edges appeared first and then the rest filled in. It was not a ghost and it was totally non-threatening. Neither did I get any sense that it was male or female. It said nothing. It did nothing. It had long hair and a long brown cloak right down to the ground. There was light surrounding the whole form. I had no reason to be frightened of it, but, because I could not work out what it was and what it was doing there, I froze with fear. So much so that it seemed forever before I could even force any sound to come out of my mouth. Eventually, I managed to scream and my father came racing into my room. As soon as he saw how frightened I was, he sent me out of the room. He never mentioned it the next day, nor did I. I have no idea what it was or why I saw it, I just know that I did. And now I some-how feel secretly pleased that I did.

A few days after that incident, my father came into my room. I thought he was coming in to discuss my decision to leave school and head for a job in the South of France. He'd had very little to say to me since that fateful day. I braced myself for the inevitable onslaught, but he just threw some-thing into the air. It landed on my bed.

"See what you think of this," was all he said.

"Okay...thanks," I said, humbly perplexed as he silently closed the door behind him.

I glanced down at the intriguing blue paper-back lying in front of me. I turned it over. There was a picture of a seagull on the front along with the words, *Jonathan Livingston Seagull*.

That book not only put out a safety net to stop my fall, it also catapulted me into a far richer life than I could possibly have imagined. Devouring each page full of words, I thought, along with the ninety million other people who read the book, that it had been written especially for me. The words seem to leap right off the page, grab me by the shoulders and shake me. Life *was* too precious to be a compromise. And compromise, as far as I was concerned, was the ultimate failure. I felt the message beckoned me on to a higher purpose...to savour the joy of living...to seek perfection. The early seeds for my spiritual quest were sown that day. My Dad had known exactly what he was doing when he'd tossed that book in my direction. I didn't realise until much later how much of himself he had shared with me on that fateful day.

When the accident had happened, I had summoned him with a scream that had reached up from the very epicentre of my being, even though he had been dead for almost a year. He had spent his whole life making things 'okay' again. Sorting out all our catastrophes.

How about this one Dad? How would your Jonathan get out of this one?

The Aborigines continued to mumble to one another and look on, as the doctor flustered around, trying to find a vein that had not collapsed.

SEVEN

Australia

There was a sound. As if someone were whispering down a long tube. It was a strange, soft, mellow sound. I tried to concentrate on the words and not the sound. The doctor was talking.

"We've done it, Tina. We've managed to get an IV into you. Now we're going to move you to the plane."

I slowly raised an eyelid. The room seemed dreamlike - all misty. A strong smell of chemicals hung in the air.

"Will it hurt?"

"No, it won't hurt, just hang on in there."

Then I remembered the severed arm.

"My *arm*!" I cried, "I'm not going without my arm! Where's my arm?"

She took hold of my right hand gently and whispered,

"Everything's okay, Christina, your arm's in a box underneath you."

The absurdity of this statement penetrated my semiconscious state, as I looked at her, and said earnestly,

"Well, I hope it doesn't pinch my bottom."

She laughed at my stupid remark. Isn't it strange how humour can infiltrate even the darkest moments?

I don't know how the plane had landed at Belyuen Aboriginal Camp. There couldn't have been a landing strip, but I have never known a bumpier take off than ours. I howled and wailed with the anguish of an animal caught in a vicious steel trap. The flight was no better once we were airborne. I tried to lie still, but felt a fluttering in my stomach each time the plane lurched. We finally bumped down and there was a flurry of activity as paramedics raced around with stretchers on wheels and flashing lights. As I looked up, I was astonished to see, that it was dark. It was night time.

"What time is it?" I enquired of one of the paramedics.

"7.30 at night, Miss."

Five hours had now passed.

* * *

I was still howling and moaning as they placed me gently onto a large hospital bed. I felt cold and the pain in my arm made me feel sick. Then, sedated, I drifted off to sleep. The curtains were left closed around my bed.

Later, Peggy, a lovely large, billowy woman with a warm Norfolk drawl, told me that she had looked across the ward to Vera, an Aboriginal woman in the bed opposite and asked, "What do you make of all that?"

"Good pair of lungs on her," Vera had replied, "the noise she was making. Probably one of those drug addicts off the street, downtown."

Some time later that night, about 1 o'clock in the morning, John Hargrave told me he had to resign himself to the fact that there was no way he could take this shredded stump and join the rest of the limb to it again. There hadn't been enough to work with. One whole muscle had completely disappeared and he'd only been able to locate one of the main nerves. The nature of the injury resembled that of one other he had dealt with. It had been a few years back when a crocodile had torn

47

off the limb of another tourist visiting the Northern Territory. In that case, he had assumed that the crocodile had eaten part of the arm – but there was no explanation as to why so much of my arm had been missing. The worst part for him, he told me, had been having to break the news to me...

"You had been so sure we'd be able to re-attach the arm. I knew you were going to take it badly."

Suddenly, the curtain surrounding the bed was swished back and a glaring spotlight at the head of the bed was switched on. I was startled out of a comfortable, drug-induced slumber. The wall light glared down, blinding me temporarily, like a spotlight used to interrogate prisoners of war.

"Where am I?" I slurred, rubbing my eyes.

I squinted and then focused on a figure in a white coat at the foot of my bed. He was speaking to me in steady, detached tones.

"Christina, we have assessed the possibility of reattaching the arm and decided that it is not possible. We will now go ahead and, after a series of debridements, form the rest of the arm into a stump suitable for a prosthesis."

I was choked back into consciousness by his cold impersonal manner. From somewhere deep within my tired, drugged body, a rage manifested itself.

"Prosthesis? What the hell is prosthesis? You..." I gulped another breath of air, "...you call yourselves doctors...in England they do these sort of operations everyday!"

I turned away from them and the light, sobbing quietly into my pillow.

Peggy had glanced over at Vera, who in turn, raised her eyebrows.

An injection was followed by darkness. The first operation was about to take place and, due to the messy nature and lengthy exposure to insects, the stump was going to take a lot of cleaning up.

John Hargrave subsequently told me that he had hoped for a cleaner wound, but there was no way he would have been able to close up this wound for some time. He hated leaving open wounds, but the risk of gangrene would have been far too high to risk closing it up at this point. It had been a game of Russian roulette. He had been forced to gamble on how much more of the gangrenous arm he could afford to leave attached before putting my life at risk. Many doctors, he'd said, would have been tempted, to go ahead and perform an above-elbow amputation. But that was the easy way out. He had seen far too many miracles happen, during his time in India doing reconstructive surgery with people suffering from leprosy, to take that route. He had wanted to save as much of the arm as was possible, even if it would take longer and be more dangerous. He'd seen what a difference that little elbow joint made to one's quality of life.

EIGHT

I opened my eyes. It was still happening. I wished this nightmare would stop and go away. There seemed to be pipes and tubes all over me, and my bandaged left arm was swinging in a sling, held onto some sort of contraption on wheels. There was a man standing over me in green overalls, wearing a hat and mask. I attempted to move but had no strength. He smiled.

"Are you my doctor?"

"No, Christina, there's your doctor over there," he said pointing in the direction of the sink.

Again, I tried to inch my way up the bed but to no avail.

"Are – are you my doctor?" I tried to shout across the room, at the man with his back to me.

He slowly turned around, and removed his mask, revealing a face brimming over with compassion. I instantly liked this tall man, in his late fifties, his slender face sporting a straw-coloured beard but no moustache.

"Yes, Christina, I am your doctor, dear."

"W...well call-family-tell-what's happened."

Without another word, John Hargrave turned towards the phone and asked for the number. As I began to drift off, I heard him talking gently and quietly into the receiver. I lay in my bed drifting in and out of sleep. The nurse came to take my blood pressure, but I did not let her see I was awake. I didn't want to be awake. I didn't want to think about what was going on, let alone have anyone else discuss it all with me. I lay absolutely still until I heard her shoes clip clopping away from the bed and back down the corridor to the nurses station.

Then, I could hold back no more. One big tear squeezed its way between my eyelashes and plopped onto my cheek. It felt cold and tickled as it ran down my feverish cheek. It all seemed so sad – so very sad. One tear followed another, tumbling down my cheek and soaking my tangled hair and pillow. Long, slow, muffled sobs issued from my mouth. I allowed my bleary gaze to wander around this alien environment in which I found myself. Never before, in my entire life had I felt more alone. Peggy had been watching me across the ward from her bed in the corner. Sorrow in the room was almost tangible. She took a deep breath and let it out slowly.

"Tina...Tina, love, are you in pain my dear?"

"No...I can hardly feel anything" I answered, my voice broken.

She took another deep breath, searching for a few words of comfort.

"Well," she began earnestly, "at least you can put your hands together and – and say you're alive, girl."

A pause ensued as the meaning of what she said began to dawn on both of us, simultaneously. I began to smile, and, as I saw the look of horror spread across her face, my smile turned into a laugh.

"That was a good one, Peggy."

Poor Peggy was still struck dumb by her inappropriate words. My cracked ribs halted the laughter suddenly, but it was certainly reassuring to learn that my sense of humour hadn't left me, along with my left hand! An injection followed...by yet another long sleep.

NINE

I slept fitfully. Days seemed to disappear, but each time I surfaced from that wonderful deep quiet ocean of sleep, I became aware of someone's presence. Whenever I moved, I felt someone taking hold of my hand and squeezing it as they whispered comforting words.

"You'll be okay, Tina," and, "Everything's going to be all right," but they all fell on deaf ears.

I have no idea how long this person had been there, or who he was, but gradually I became more aware of his comforting words. Finally, after Jamie Mann had been sitting there for forty-eight hours, I opened both eyes and stared right at him.

"Hi! Welcome back!"

"Who – who are you?" I slurred at this man who seemed to be extremely familiar with me, "Why are you here, with me?"

I was confused.

"Well Tina, I was on my way to Katherine in my four-wheeler when your story was flashed across on the radio. I don't know what made me do it – but I just had this compelling desire to turn my jeep around. On the way here, I called by the store and got you a toothbrush, hairbrush and a night-dress. I have been meditating, whilst sitting here at the side of your bed, trying to send healing, positive energy to you whilst you slept. I hope you don't mind."

He pointed to a book and a tape on my bedside table. They were entitled *Alpha-Thinking* by Jess Stearn.

"Don't look so dubious. There's nothing to be frightened about. When you are feeling a little better, you may like to read through this book to see what it is all about."

He placed it on my locker, beside my bed.

I summoned up a polite smile, but at that moment, there was nothing I felt less like doing than reading his book. Sensing that he was moving too rapidly, he stood up, clumsily fishing about in his trouser pocket, finally producing a small enamel brooch.

"Look," he said, pressing it into my hand, "I've just had these things made for the members of my meditation group. I want you to have one."

It was a tiny rainbow, springing forth from a fluffy, white cloud. I closed my fingers around it, as though it were the Hope Diamond. To this day, it goes everywhere with me. Jamie left me to rest.

"Your boyfriend gone then, love?" Peggy called across the ward.

"He's not my boyfriend, Peg!" I laughed.

"He's not? Well who is he then? He seemed extremely attentive."

"I don't even know him, Peggy...never seen him before in my life."

I dozed off. The excitement of it all was just too much. I slept on and off throughout the rest of the day and much of the night; stirring only for an injection or dressing change.

TEN

The next few days were confusing and my memory is very vague. I recall Jamie being there. I remember his wife coming one day to wash my hair. It was an interesting experience having one's hair washed, lying horizontally in bed, pumped up with some kind of heroin-based pain killing drug. I remember smiling distractedly, as she pulled a significant-sized piece of twig from my skull. I'd been so heavily drugged I had felt nothing. Blood was caked all around it.

I felt as if I were swimming – drifting – even drowning. Every so often, the drugs would wear off enough for my mind to clear away the mists and come up for breath – even hold a conversation. But these times were limited; I much preferred swimming through my drug-induced Avalon.

I have no recollection of any visitors, apart from Jamie. Although I later found out that there had been several. One was a lady from Scarborough, North Yorkshire. Her letter, with full descriptions of my flaming red hair strewn across the pillow and my blood-scarred face, really disturbed me. The woman wrote as if she knew me well. I didn't know her at all.

It is humbling to imagine that strangers were bothered enough about my plight to pay me a visit. Everybody wrote and sent flowers and cards. Prayers were said in Northallerton, as well as in the school where I worked. I was told that some children were so distraught that they had to return home. It amazes me to think that these children were so concerned.

* * *

At the time of the accident, I was wilfully devoid of spirituality – God, or otherwise. I was still very raw from the experience of my father's death. I felt as if I'd pleaded, begged and screamed to every corner of the Universe to give me a reason for his death and had received no response whatsoever. I could hardly go near a church without tears welling up behind my eyelids. The main point I want to make is where I stood spiritually when all this occurred. It was not a pretty place. I certainly did not merit this wave of spiritual power that seemed to be manifesting itself and engulfing me.

One of the most horrendous times was when they came to change the dressing. The arm had been torn off and, due to the prolonged exposure to tropical heat and insects, it had become badly infected. It was therefore impossible for them to risk closing up the wound at this stage. If closed, the infection would spread to the bone and that could be fatal. So, the only thing they could do was to keep the wound open and try to prevent the arm from rotting away by removing the dressing twice daily, and irrigating the open wound and bone with some kind of disinfecting solution. It was hell. I know other people have suffered far worse atrocities than this and my heart aches for anyone who has suffered in this manner, but for me, this was as close to hell as I hope I ever get.

At this point, I couldn't even look at the stump whilst it was still bandaged, but *this*...this was like being permanently joined to a living horror movie of the worst kind. Straight after dressing, there was maybe an hour when I felt reasonably calm, but gradually, I began to think about the next one.

My heart began to beat so fast and loud that my whole body seemed to pound with it. My mind was so befuddled that I couldn't focus on anything but the next unveiling. Cold sweat, produced from fear, dripped down my body. By the time the nurse pulled those curtains around my bed to start again, I was soaked. I never knew the real meaning of hell, until that time. Black is the only appropriate word.

At times, I used to hallucinate. The stump would become alive. A writhing, snake-like creature joined to the end of my arm. In abject panic, I would slam my hand hard down on the emergency call button and a nurse would appear, breathless at the foot of my bed.

"What's the matter Christina?"

Beckoning her towards me with a shaking finger, I would hiss, "What's this? What is this?"...pointing to the writhing creature on the end of my arm.

"Christina, love, it's your arm...don't you remember? You had an accident..."

Then I would awaken from my hell and, placated once again, I'd slip back into those sweet, cool mists.

It was after one such episode that I lay in my bed, breathless and numb, seriously wondering how much more of this I could endure. I truly didn't believe that I could take it for much longer. Everything seemed so hopeless and ugly.

People talk about turning points. This was mine. Someone had brought me a 'Get-Well' card. On the front of it was a beautiful painting of the bridge at Argenteuil by Monet. I fixated on it for hour upon hour. Someone had stuck it to the footboard of my bed. I stared at the colours, the abundance of purple colour in the ripples of the water, every shade of purple under the sun. It was this card and this card alone that came to represent the only 'good' left in my world. I had to hang on to it. I *had* to hang on to it. Mere words cannot convey what this little card did for me. Even now, I cannot talk about it without tears welling up in my eyes and my throat becoming constricted. Whilst drowning in horror, the beauty of this little painting reached out, cutting through the darkness, and threw me a lifeline to clutch on to, and clutch on to it I did. Thank God for Monet!

ELEVEN

One day I awoke to the sounds of shrieking. It appeared to be coming from the next ward. I was shaken by these anguished screams. They were filled with panic and terror, but the reason I was so moved was because they were coming from the mouth of a child. A nurse was busying herself at the foot of my bed.

"Sister," I mumbled one day.

"Yes, Christina." she replied.

"Those screams...I heard them yesterday, too. Who is it screaming?"

"It's a little aboriginal girl, Christina. She got caught in a bush fire...her skirt caught alight. She's burnt from the waist down. Each morning she has to be immersed in a saline solution."

I sank my head back down into the pillow. The deep sorrow I felt for that small child was almost tangible. It was then that I swore an oath to myself never to wallow in self-pity. My injury was nothing compared to that tiny child in the next room.

* * *

I was coming round from my second operation, when the nurse interrupted my reverie...

"Christina."

"Umm?" was all I could reply.

"Christina, guess what? Your Mum's arriving tonight. She should be here when you wake up tomorrow."

I let out a long, slow breath of sheer relief.

The thought that soon I would be seeing her was the best news I could have had. At last, I would not be alone. Everyone had been marvellous, but, somehow, I still felt alone. I wasn't sure what was happening to me. They still hadn't sewn up my arm, so obviously things weren't progressing as well as they should. I was tired of facing all this stuff alone. I just wanted a big hug from my Mum. It would be wonderful to know she was there. I wasn't up to much talking, preferring to swim around in my silvery mists, but just knowing she was there was going to be great. I tried to imagine what her mental state would be like. It was almost the first anniversary of my father's death. Nobody had dreamt that this was how we were going to be spending it. God! How guilty I felt, to be putting her through yet more misery.

TWELVE

Darwin Hospital

"Tina, your mum's going to be here in an hour. She's just phoned to see how you were. I'm not going to give you your injection until just before she comes, so that it will last a bit longer...okay."

"Yes...now when she comes, I want to be standing up."

"Now don't be silly, Christina. I don't think it's a good idea to be moving about so soon, do you?"

"I want to be standing up!"

The nurse had now come to recognise that stubborn tone in my voice and knew that debating, any further with this hot-headed little 'Brit' would be a waste of time. Compromise was the only way to negotiate with this one.

"Well, how about we put you in the little 'family room' with your drips. You can sit in there and wait until she comes...ay? I've got some make-up in my bag. We can give you a wash, brush your hair and put a lick of make up on. How about that, then?"

"Could you? Oh, that would be great!"

So, the nurse set about washing me, carefully brushing my head, still full of painful cuts. By the time they loaded me into the wheelchair and pushed me into the 'family room', I felt wonderful. Sitting upright took some getting used to. I didn't want to look too ill when she walked in. I thought the nurse had done quite a good job of covering the cuts on my face.

Even though the door was slightly ajar and I was expecting my mother to walk through it, it was a shock when she did. I was sitting with a great big smile on my face.

The door swung open and she stood there smiling, I mustered every ounce of strength to get to my feet.

She paused a moment in the doorway, silently appraising the situation.

"It's all right, Mum," I said, "I've only lost my arm."

She rushed forward, wrapping her arms around me.

"Hey, hey...be careful. Mind my tubes," I said, lowering myself back into my seat.

I was trying so hard to be cheerful. What I really wanted to do was to sob in her arms.

"Tell me about your trip, Mum. Did it go on forever?"

It had been still dark when Mum's plane had turned onto its final approach path into Darwin International Airport. She told me that, even though it had been a long, long flight, she could scarcely remember any of it. This had been her first flight outside Europe and she had looked as cool as a cucumber. She realised that, if she had thought too much, she would not have been able to cope. The plane had been boarded by customs officials who sprayed pesticide through-out the plane. She had been appalled. She managed to cover her eyes and nose just in time, before she had been enveloped in the foul spray.

She had been shocked when she made her way through the door of the aircraft and was hit in the face by air as hot as a steaming flannel. The humidity had been suffocating.

Finally, after lots of questions and a long, sweaty wait, she had pushed her suitcase through the automatic doors and into the arrivals area. There had been no familiar faces, nobody rushing forward. She had kept going through the arrivals area and out of the door. The heat had hit her once again. She found she was forced to breathe short, shallow breaths. It was lighter now. There had been a line of about four or five cabs right outside the airport. She had turned the corner, her heart pounding rapidly, and noticed an old bench facing the road. She lugged her case to a nearby bench and flopped down on it.

All the taxis filled up and drew away from the kerb.

Quite suddenly, the busy airport was completely empty, save for an elderly man in a uniform, who was locking up. She had no idea where she was going, or what she was going to do next. She was exhausted by now and merely gazed ahead of her at the dry wilderness that was now humbly revealing itself to her, as the giant sun began to climb over the horizon for the start of another day. Everything had felt so alien to her. She'd distractedly followed the path of a clumsy cockroach, working its way along the gutter. The dry, cracked land, with the burnt grass hanging desperately to its roots, looked ruthless. Everything seemed to be threatening and barren. She hadn't been able to cry. Fatigue had gripped her tired body and confused mind. She'd just sat on the bench swinging her feet and watching the world, but seeing nothing. The knuckles of her right hand were white, as she'd continued to clasp the handle of her suitcase, as if her very life had depended on it. One thought had kept niggling at her consciousness. 'What, in hell's name was she doing here?'

A car had pulled up and a painfully thin girl hung out of the window. Mum had looked again, hoping that it was Pauline, but no way could this be the fresh-faced girl who usually appeared to be bouncing with health. This woman, mere skin and bone, looked drawn and tired. Her mass of luscious red curls had gone. She was out of the car now and awkwardly approaching Mum. It *had* been her, but Mum hardly recognised the girl she had known since birth.

Her mind had slipped back into happier times when she and Pauline's mother first discovered that they were expecting us. They had been close friends for several years. Frieda had two children and was now expecting the arrival of the third. One day, she had been bemoaning the fact that she had to attend the ante-natal clinic, when my mother told her that she would join her.

"No...no, you don't have to do that, Lau," she had replied, thinking that this was an offer of support.

"You don't understand, Frieda," she'd said, "I'm going to the clinic too...I have to...I have an appointment!"

It had taken a few minutes for the full meaning of my mother's statement to fully register.

"Wait...you mean you have to go? Yer wee devil...how long have you known?"

"Oh...about the same amount of time as you..." my mother grinned, sheepishly, "...I wanted to be absolutely sure this time before telling anyone."

Frieda had been dumbstruck. How could she have kept this to herself all this time? She had known how desperately Laura and Tony had wanted a child. This was great news. She let out a shriek and sent a cushion hurtling through the air at my mother.

It turned out that the two babies were due about the same time. Years later, Frieda's daughter, Pauline and I had joked later that we both happened to come along nine months after a particularly good New Year's Eve party...we were with a Scottish Regiment after all!

The sound of her name had brought her back to the present. It had been Pauline in the car.

"God...sorry we're late, Laura, our alarm clock didn't go off...I don't *believe* the bloody thing," she'd said to Mum.

"How's Tina?" was all Mum could say.

Pauline had told her that I was fine and dropped her off at the hospital.

I had wanted to talk more but felt myself fading fast. I had to go back to bed for a rest.

"Can you get the nurse to bring the wheelchair?" I said to Mum.

My energy came and went in fits and spurts these days. I was placed back in bed and, promptly fell fast asleep, leaving my mother still holding the few notes and presents she brought from well-wishers back home.

A few hours later, I woke up. Mum was still sitting by my bed.

"Hello there," she said, "How are you feeling?'

"Much better. Tell me what's been happening at home. How's Dave?"

"Well, did you know that it was Dave who first received the phone call from that headmaster in Australia?"

"No, where were you?"

"I was on a bus going to see your Uncle in London. The police were waiting for me at Victoria Station and told me to call Dave immediately. At first, I thought it was old Uncle Son. I had this picture of him being found on the floor of his little flat. The police took me to the station and let me call Dave. He didn't want to tell me over the phone. He just kept telling me that you'd had an accident and that I was to come home immediately. He met me at Northallerton station and I insisted that he told me there and then what was going on. He looked dreadful, 'Teen, all ashen grey and white round the gills. He put his arm around me and said, 'Teen's had an accident. When I got the first phone call, she had only just been found, somewhere in the Australian Outback. I've just rung Darwin Hospital to see how she was doing and they told me that she hadn't yet arrived, but the plane is on it's way to get her. I can't understand what's taking them so long.'

He had paused, taking a deep breath then he told me, 'Mum...*her arm has been pulled off in the accident.*'

His words hit me like bullets, 'Teen. I couldn't breathe. We both stood there supporting each other and sobbing on the platform of the old station."

It seemed strangely gratifying to hear how deeply affected my brother had been. We were never ones to be over emotional. Now, I realised just how much I meant to him. It was a warm and comforting feeling to know how much he cared. In fact, he proved to be one of my greatest supports in the years following the accident.

THIRTEEN

A couple of days after my mother's arrival, it was announced that the arm was becoming seriously infected again, and I was to have yet a third debridement operation the following day. It was becoming absurd. Every day or so, I was raced back into the operating theatre for another operation. When I awoke, the arm was shorter. It was impossible for me to start to come to terms with the situation when my arm was a different shape and size every other day.

On occasions, when I came round, I was frightened to take a look at the bandaged arm, swinging at the side of my bed, on the metal frame, because I feared that it would be gone altogether. I had no idea until much later that I was critically ill and that it had been touch-and-go for a while there. I hallucinated a lot; imagining cockroaches were crawling about on the sheets in my bed and insisting on a complete change of bed linen. One time, I woke up screaming dementedly for the nurse. Within seconds she appeared, breathless, at my bedside.

"What's wrong Christina?" she panted.

I lent forward, and whispered in her ear,

"You know that special shampoo you put on the aborigines' hair to get rid of nits?"

"Yes."

"Well, I want you to wash my hair with it right now," I commanded.

"But Christina, you haven't got any nits...why would we do that?"

"Yes, yes I have," I hissed, " I can hear them...jumping...in my hair."

It seems strange, but until I'd actually heard myself saying these things, I didn't realise how stupid they sounded. It was as though, by verbalising them, I broke the hallucinatory spell.

The aborigines in my ward would watch these scenes from their beds, amused, I'm sure, at the strange behaviour of the eccentric 'Brit'.

One time, I awoke to find myself in a totally different ward – in a bed, all on my own. I remember feeling panicky, because my bed had been facing a different way from that to which I was accustomed. Nobody was around. The room was grey, with a large window. The beams of light, tumbling through that window, were blinding. I squinted and rubbed my eyes, raising them upwards to the domed ceiling. It was like that of a great arched cathedral. There was a beautiful, white bird circling inside the dome. With each circle, it came nearer to me. I wondered if it were Jonathan. Finally, it came to rest on my shoulder. Then I knew I was about to fly. Without waiting a second, I sprang up into the air. The bird flew alongside. Together we swooped and circled around the inside of the ceiling. I became lost in my freedom – dancing joyously through the air. I looked around for Jonathan, but he had gone. So had the brilliant light and the vaulted ceiling. I panicked and found myself falling through the air, no longer able to fly. I wasn't particularly frightened. I just felt more annoyed that everything had gone. I fell into a restless sleep. When I awoke, I was, mysteriously, back in my old ward.

"Oh!" I said to one of the nurses, "you've put me back in this ward."

"What d'you mean Christina?" She'd said.

"Well, that other room was beautiful, but it was a bit lonely on my own, and the bed was around the wrong way."

"Christina, love, you haven't been anywhere. You've been here all the time."

"No, no," I insisted. "It must have been when you weren't on duty. I was in this other room...I was...you know," I said, pleadingly.

"You've been very sick for the last two days, darl. Haven't heard your blinking Pommie accent for a while," she giggled, tidying my bed.

I glanced around the ward. Over the other side, was my mother, sitting by Peggy's bed giving her a foot-massage.

"Great hospital visitor you are," I joked, "visiting everybody in the hospital except your own daughter."

My mum looked around. She looked pale and sallow.

"Well, I wasn't going to spend all day looking at your closed eyelids. You haven't surfaced for two days."

I was just starting to enjoy this banter when a severe looking nurse approached my bed.

"Come on now, Christina, time to get that dressing changed."

"Oh God, no, not again."

This wiped the relaxed smile clean off my face. My heart zipped into overdrive and the sweat began to accumulate all over my body. The curtain swished closed round the bed and the gas and air cylinder was wheeled to my bedside.

"First things first, eh," she said, whipping the bedclothes back and sticking a needle deep into my thigh.

"We'll give that a few minutes to work while I'm getting everything ready. Now try to keep calm, Christina."

'Was it me, or did I detect a sign of nerves in the nurse?' I thought, as I began to swim again, through those wonderful numbing mists.

"Mrs Sadler, would you mind giving me a hand, during the dressing."

"No, not at all." replied my mother.

My heart sank. The nurse stood on the left of the bed and Mum found a chair and sat on the right. She was told to try and stop my injured arm from jerking as the antiseptic solution was poured over the open wound. The gas and air mask was placed over my face. I inhaled deeply and stared at my mother's face as the dressings were slowly and gently removed from my stump.

I hadn't seen the mess on the end of my arm yet, and even though it was the last thing I wanted to see, I was curious. I knew it was bad. I could tell by the way the nurses acted when they had to do the dressing, but I had no idea just how grotesque it actually looked.

I scrutinised my mother's eyes, as the last piece of gauze was removed. I knew her eyes were looking directly at the rotting stump and I wanted to see it through her eyes, but not my own. The more anxious I became, the faster I sucked in lungfuls of gas and air.

Suddenly a young nurse pushed her way through my curtains saying, as she came in, "Hey, Sister Matthews, d'you know where the...," her eyes suddenly moved, from the face of the nurse down to my open wound.

"Shit!" she exclaimed, a look of horror on her face, as she recoiled out through the curtains once more "Sorry!"

"Oh, Christ!" I thought to myself, "...it must be appalling, if trained nurses are horrified by the sight of it."

The first nurse continued, attempting to disregard the previous scene. My mother sat there with a calm expression on her smiling face, but her eyes betrayed her. She couldn't hide the horror she was witnessing. I could see it in her eyes. I inhaled the gas and air...faster and faster. Everybody else was too involved in the procedure to monitor my intake of the gas and air.

Off I went on one of my dream flights. Once I'd escaped reality, it was quite fun. I swooped and floated back up and rolled around. It was wonderful. Then all of a sudden my swim was interrupted by the foulest language imaginable. I was horrified to hear such bad language being bandied around. To me, it sounded as if it were coming down a long, hollow tube of some kind. I hated listening to it. It spoilt my dreaming.

Then, someone was removing the gas and air mask and tapping me on the face.

"Christina, it's all over now. It's done now."

I opened my eyes and looked towards my Mum, who was sitting there, dumbstruck.

"Did you hear all that swearing?"

"Yes, I certainly did!" she said all tight-lipped.

"Well, who was it? Where was it coming from?" I said, edging towards her as if I were about to partake of a nice juicy piece of gossip...

"You know very well where it was coming from...I didn't know you knew such words."

"What? Are you telling me that I was the one swearing?"

She nodded.

"Oh, my God...how embarrassing!" I cried.

The curtains were pushed back and everyone in the ward was silent – looking at me in astonishment, their jaws hanging open.

Perhaps this sweet little Brit wasn't Mary Poppins, after all.

FOURTEEN

Days and nights all drifted into one. On occasions, I would hit it just right, and be lively for a short while during the daytime, but mostly I awoke about 2 or 3 in the morning. My mind would be quite clear and there was a short time, in between painkilling drugs, when not only would my mind ring clear, but also, I had little pain. These were golden little moments. I would open my eyes and glance around the room to check out where I was.

The strange thing about these times was that there was an aboriginal girl in the bed opposite mine. It didn't matter when I opened my eyes, she would be propped up in bed staring across at me. Her stare didn't falter, even when she saw that I was staring right back. All I could see, through the murky darkness of the room, were the whites of her eyes – and her teeth – glistening through the darkness. More often than not, she said nothing. I found it quite alarming at times. Her name was Denise. She died shortly after her trip to hospital and one is not supposed to refer to the departed by name, for fear of disturbing their spirit, but it's been several years since her death, so I think I'm allowed to use her name. I never felt frightened by her. I always felt that she was somehow protecting me. We spoke very little, but when I got to know her, I found her to be a gentle soul with a mischievous sense of humour. Sometimes, when she felt well enough, she used to perform 'corroborree' dances, sacred dances, at the foot of my bed.

Apparently, to do this was sacrilegious. The other aborigines used to come and drag her off to a corner and scold her.

But she would still come back and do it, time and time again.

"Dis one called 'Pig Under Der Mango Tree'..." and off she would go again with impressions of a pig that had eaten too many mangos, and now was suffering the consequences.

She would furtively keep glancing around, to ascertain that Alfie, an aboriginal man, wasn't around to catch her. Alfie almost had to have his hand amputated after smashing it against a wall whilst trying to fight some spirits who had been taunting him. Alfie and I both had the same neurosurgeon. One day, Dr Hargrave turned up during breakfast to see if I had learnt to butter toast with one hand yet. He swished back the curtains from round my bed, plonked himself down on it, shouting out, "Amazing...isn't she just amazing?" or, "How's my beautiful Brit this morning?"

Of course, I knew that these energetic exaltations were nothing more than a ploy on his part, to give me a boost...but I loved his visits and looked forward to them.

Another time I woke to find a preacher praying over me.

"Oh God", I thought, "It's finally happened!"

The preacher, a wiry Irishman in his fifties, saw the look of alarm on my face and quickly explained what he was doing. He'd been coming to me regularly to pray for my 'safe deliverance', but had never found me awake – so couldn't introduce himself.

He was a kindly man, but I was astounded when he asked earnestly, "Christina, would you be wanting your arm to have a proper burial?"

I started to laugh, but noticed he wasn't laughing with me.

"Sometimes people like to have their amputated limbs buried...in a proper fashion."

I looked at him and laughed again. What an absurd thought.

"No, thank you...but nice of you to ask."

There was another man of God in the hospital, Father Tom. Father Tom was a handsome young man. His dark sultry looks led me to believe he had some aboriginal blood running through his veins. Rather like me, now, I mused. I'd already had several substantial blood transfusions and was most reliably informed, that much of the blood collected by the transfusion service in Australia was sold to them by aborigines. I'm rather proud to have the blood of such a noble race coursing through my veins. Anyway, Father Tom and the Pastor seemed to be trying to out do each other on their hospital rounds. Whenever I was about to be taken down for an operation, both would appear, breathless, at the side of my bed and begin praying for my safe deliverance. I didn't mind this, though. As I said to my mother, when she told me that someone had invited her to go to church one Sunday, and she hadn't felt much like thanking God for her life at that particular moment:

"Go, Mum...for God's sake go! There might be something in it...there might not...but at this moment in time, we can't afford to take any more chances. If you don't buy a raffle ticket, you don't stand a chance of winning the prize."

She had laughed and gone along to church.

FIFTEEN

It had been a while since I last had an operation, and the fact that I hadn't been rushed down to the theatre for a fourth operation meant that the steady flood of antibiotics, flowing into my right arm, were beginning to win their struggle. If my progress kept up like this, I was told, they would be able to think about closing up the wound.

There was nothing more I wanted in the whole world than this.

* * *

By now, I was beginning to take more notice of the people who came to visit.

One day, I was awakened to see a friend of Peter and Pauline's. Andrew was a tall, thin man with long jet-black hair and large, intense blue eyes. I was surprised to see him, because I didn't feel that I'd had much of a chance to make his acquaintance during the five days preceding that fateful day. He was an easy-going, sensitive type with a quiet disposition. He pulled up a chair and looked deeply into my eyes,

"How are you?"

He looked so sad that I felt I had to lighten the situation. We talked about the day before the accident, when several of us had gone off riding Peter's motorbikes. I had already forgotten about it. I smiled as he reminded me about all the fun we had enjoyed together.

" Andrew," I said, "...d'you know what bugs me more than anything else about the accident?"

"What's that?"

"I've lost my watch...and I love that watch."

He looked up and around the room, almost with a look of embarrassment. Then he looked down at his feet again.

"Tina," he said slowly, "never mind your watch...you've lost your arm, Tina, don't you realise...you've lost an arm?"

"Of course I do, Andrew," I laughed, "but that watch was very special to me. It was on my left arm, along with an emerald ring. I'm forever losing that watch. I mean...I *lose* it, but it always comes back to me, one way or another."

My parents had given it to me when I graduated from college. I treasured that watch, but it didn't take long before I had 'misplaced' it. Shortly afterwards, it turned up again, under my pillow...but this set a precedent...the watch went missing...and then it turned up...usually in the most peculiar places. In the refrigerator, or in a plant pot. Once, I lost it for two whole months. I didn't panic initially, because I knew it would turn up. But as the weeks went by, I began to lose faith. I tidied my car and scoured my bedroom, but to no avail. Finally, as a last resort, I rang the police.

"This is Christina Sadler," I said, "I've lost a Seiko watch. You haven't had it handed in, have you?"

"When was the watch lost, Miss Sadler?"

"Well, actually, it's been gone for about two months now," I spluttered, knowing how absurd it sounded.

Silence ensued.

Then the amused man asked,

"You don't drink in the Green Tree Pub, do you?"

I was quite affronted by this seemingly irrelevant question.

"Well, I have been known to drink there, yes, but I haven't been there for a long time, why?"

"Well," came the reply, "they've had a Seiko watch behind the bar there for nearly two months, hoping someone would

claim it. Since it hasn't been claimed, they brought it into us...that was just two days ago."

I was overjoyed. I knew it was my watch and raced down to the station to reclaim it.

"So, you see, Andrew, the watch has a special place in my heart. Now it's gone for good, and my arm with it. I got the emerald ring back. It's in the drawer, there," I nodded my head towards my locker drawer, "...but they tell me that the ring is badly damaged and the emerald itself is shattered. I can't bring myself to look at it because I know precisely how they got the ring off the finger. I keep visualising the whole gory procedure taking place, dispassionately...as if they were cutting off someone else's finger to retrieve someone else's battered ring. I wish they had left it where it belonged. The hand is probably nothing more than a pile of ashes now, and the thought of them cutting off my finger to get the ring shouldn't matter, but it does, Andrew...don't ask me why, but it does. I'll never be able to wear the ring again."

Andrew was an astute person. His eyes clouded over and he bid me his fond farewell.

A couple of days later, Andrew walked back into my ward again. He lent over me and whispered

"Hi!"

I stirred and opened my eyes.

"Andrew," I mumbled.

There was something different about his demeanour. He had a triumphant smile upon his face. I rubbed my eyes and looked over at him again. He was reaching deep into his trench coat pocket.

'Oh, good, he has brought me more chocolate,' I thought.

He withdrew his hand from his pocket and dangled a small

plastic bag before my eyes. I squinted and focused on the bag, trying to make out it's contents.

No...it couldn't be. *It was!*

There, in the bag was the face of my very own watch – no wristband – no glass – but the familiar old face was there – battered and scratched but still working. I couldn't believe my eyes.

It had happened again!

Following his last visit, Andrew explained that he had left the hospital, jumped into his car and driven the hundred or so miles to the scene of the accident. The sight that met his eyes was one of utter devastation. The ground was littered with fragments of glass and bent pieces of metal. He looked about in dismay. There was no way he was going to be able to find the watch in these blood-splattered ruins. Turning to get into his car, he noticed something glistening on the ground. He was just about to flick it into the air with his foot, when he stopped. He bent down to examine it, and, sure enough, it was my watch – no wristband or glass. Just the face...and it was still going. Things were looking up.

SIXTEEN

I'd been in hospital for what seemed like a long time when something dawned on me. There had been lots of kind people come to visit me – but someone was missing. Margot hadn't, to my knowledge, been to see me. This worried me because I had been told that Dina, her daughter had sustained a badly broken leg, during the accident, and that she was in the ward right above mine.

My mind kept trying to make excuses. 'Maybe she was too busy with Dina, maybe she was too tired'...but in my heart I knew that there had to be more to it than this. She had to pass my ward every day. Surely, she could have popped in for two minutes. Something was wrong. I started to feel guilty. Maybe Margot blames me for the accident and Dina breaking her leg. If it hadn't been for me, they wouldn't have gone on the trip. This was all my fault.

Then, as if she had heard my thoughts, that very afternoon, I was half-asleep, just lying in bed staring across at Denise, when something caught my eye. I turned to see what it was, and there was Margot, standing in the entrance to the ward. She looked at me and I looked at her, but neither of us could speak. She walked towards me, still in silence and stood by my bed.

"I – I don't know what to say," she spluttered.

"There's nothing to say, Margot. It's nobody's fault. Just one of those things – and we're all alive – that's the main thing. Come here," I said, trying to give her a hug.

I felt much easier, once I'd seen her.

Dina's leg fracture had been a messy one. She had

smashed the growing part of the leg bone and so would have to have several operations to lengthen the bone as she grew. Little Dina and I would have a reminder of that day for the rest of our natural lives. My guilt was further compounded a few days later when a policeman arrived at the ward.

"Do you feel up to giving a police report?" The nurse said.

"Yes, I don't mind," I replied.

I tried to answer his questions as fully as I could, but there were great big gaps in my memory. I was pleased I'd managed to make it clear that... Yes, we were all wearing our seat belts... Yes, the windows were up (we were using the air-conditioner). No, Margot had not been speeding...and no, there had been no alcohol consumed before or during the journey. No, I did not know that the insurance was due to run out the day after the accident. I was merely the passenger, I had to remind him.

The policeman sighed, closed his book and looked at me.

"You know, you're a very, very lucky girl. I went out to look at the car yesterday. I've not seen many people walk away from accidents like that. Are you sure nothing's wrong with your legs? Only a couple of scratches on the knee? D'you mind if I look at your legs? Jesus! You're right...I can't believe it...where did you put them? There's nothing left of the front left of the car...the seat and bonnet are mashed together now, like a concertina...no gap between them...by rights you shouldn't have any legs either, girl. It's a miracle that you're still here."

He looked up and saw that I now appeared to be shaking and pale.

"Well, thank you for your help Christina. I know it couldn't have been easy."

He moved his chair back and went to leave.

"Oh, by the way," he called back over his shoulder, "the tree you hit was called an Iron-Bark tree...it lived up to it's name didn't it? I hate to tell you this...but there's hardly a scratch on it."

I wish he hadn't told me that...

I felt like going back and chopping the damned thing down.

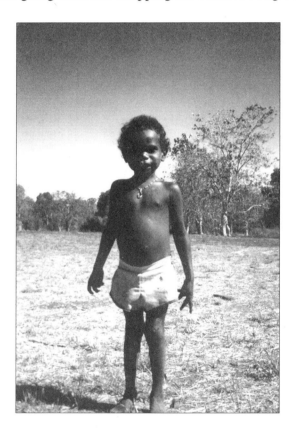

SEVENTEEN

One day, about three or four weeks after the accident, Dr Hargrave stopped and sat on the edge of my bed.

"So how are we today?" he asked, "Nurse tells me that you've been hallucinating an awful lot lately."

"Yes, Doctor, I keep imagining stuff is crawling all over my body and so I scratch it off quickly – but because I can't feel my skin all that well because of all the drugs, I usually take off a few layers before I start to feel anything...and I seem to pour with blood when I do this. My blood doesn't seem to coagulate very quickly, now. It ruins the sheets. It's driving me mad."

"Well, Christina, you've been responding very well to the antibiotics. We've got rid of almost all the gangrene without you losing too much more of your arm. I now feel that we've done as much as we can here. I want you to have the best of all possible treatment and, for that to happen, we need to close up your wound with a graft of skin, probably from your thigh. It'll take at least two operations for us to have grafted enough onto the stump ...then we will have you all ready to ship back to England, where I know you will get the best treatment."

I sat up, sharply stunned at his words.

"No!" I wailed, "No...I want you to do it all. I want to stay here forever...I don't want to go back...please don't make me go back," I sobbed.

"Christina! Christina, I'm quite willing to do the work here, but I know that you won't be getting the best treatment in the world. I'm recommending that you go see a certain

Consultant at the Royal National Orthopaedic in London. He is a leader in this sort of surgery...at the forefront of his field."

"Noooo!" I wailed, "I don't want to leave you."

"Well, think it over, dear. We'll talk further on this matter later...there's still a few hurdles to go through before a decision needs to be made. Nurse, I want this catheter and urine bag removed. I also want to see how Christina responds to a lower dose of *Omnopon*." (an opiate pain- killer)

As he was busy dispensing all these instructions, Alfie sauntered into the ward.

"Alfie, come over here," smiled Dr Hargrave.

"Do you mind sharing your washroom with Christina? I'm going to let her start walking around a little now."

Alfie's eyes sparkled with respect for this great doctor. He shook his head,

"No, Doc – I don' mind."

I was ecstatic. All of a sudden all sorts of possibilities presented themselves. I wouldn't have an awful urine bag. I wouldn't have to balance precariously upon a bedpan. I would be able to shower instead of having bed baths. Now Alfie wouldn't be the only mobile one in the ward.

"Now don't over do it Christina. You're still very weak. I just want you to build yourself up before the final operations."

"Okay, I won't." I grinned mischievously.

As soon as he'd gone, the nurse came over to my bed.

"So *you're* Christina." I looked up.

"Yes, why?"

"Well you have a lot to answer for, my girl."

Only the impish sparkle in her eyes told me she wasn't really angry with me.

"What have I done?"

"Well, for one thing, because of you, my husband was dragged from his bed in the middle of the night...he was the orthopaedic surgeon who helped to rebuild your elbow joint and fused the end of the two bones together."

I didn't realise that the bones had been fused together.

"Yes...and it took him all night to do it."

"Well, tell him I certainly appreciate it."

"That's not all...That Friday happened to be my first time back in nursing after a fourteen years. I left to bring up my kids, you know. Anyway, when you were flown in, I was sent to help out...and what did they do? They only gave me your amputated arm to carry up to theatre, didn't they! Without warning, it was placed in my arms. I tell you, I almost walked right back out the hospital there and then. You were almost responsible for the shortest ever career in nursing."

I was suddenly very interested.

"Nurse, what did it look like? I mean, was it all smashed up? Were all my fingers still on it?"

I couldn't believe I was asking these questions.

"Well, odd as it may seem, apart from being very bloated and slightly blue, it looked almost perfect to me. Smelt awful, though. Almost made me throw up. The little finger was a little crushed...but not all that much...but you know what upset me most? There was a lovely emerald ring glistening on one of the fingers. Made it look quite eerie. Did you ever get it back?"

"Er, yes. It's in that draw," I nodded my head towards my bedside locker, "...but I haven't been able to look at it yet."

"Haven't you?"

She went to pull the drawer open; "I'll get it out for you."

"No...I haven't been able to look at it...because I don't want to yet. Do you understand?"

She slid the drawer closed again.

"Yes, I guess I do, my love...everything in it's own time, eh? Everything in it's own time."

She started to dismantle some of my tubes.

"Can I have a shower nurse?"

"I don't see why not. Sit up for a while first, so you can get used to being vertical once again. I'm going to find some plastic, so I can cover that stump of yours. We can't get that wet, can we?"

Even the use of that awful word 'stump' couldn't dampen my spirits. Yippee! Thirty minutes later, I was shuffling along, on wobbly legs towards Alfie's shower room. It seemed strange, sharing my washroom with a great, big, black aborigine. I hoped he didn't mind my intrusion into his previously private domain. I felt like a baby colt trying to make its first tentative steps. It had been a long time since I'd had to walk. We made it to the shower, my arm wrapped up tightly in a clear plastic bag, like a piece of meat in a supermarket.

"Do you want to go in on your own?" the nurse asked.

"Of course I do...you don't think I want anyone to see me like this?" I laughed.

She set the temperature and I stepped into the shower. It was bliss. I can't tell you how good it felt to feel this water running all over my body. I stood there motionless for a few minutes just savouring the moment. Then I set about the business of washing. It didn't take me long to admit that trying to wash using one arm with a drip still joined to it was virtually impossible. I couldn't reach the parts I used to!! Sensing a problem, the nurse, who was still standing guard, outside, shouted,

"Hey, Pomme! D'yer need a hand?"

On hearing me laugh inside the cubicle, she realised what she'd said.

"Oh my God-I'm so sorry-I-I didn't mean ..."

"I know, I know," I laughed "...but it was funny, wasn't it?"

The next day I seriously needed to use the bathroom. Alfie was in there. He seemed to live in there. Finally, he appeared at the doorway.

"Okay if I go in, Alfie?" I said.

"Sure...I finished now."

I swung my legs round in the bed and started to make my wobbly way to the loo. Several minutes later, on reaching for the paper, I found I had a problem tearing it off. You wouldn't imagine that you need two hands to tear toilet paper, would you?

After pondering upon this matter, I had a brain wave. Stick it under the arm pit, then pull. It worked a treat. I got up, feeling quite triumphant and wandered back, through the whole ward, to my bed.

When I finally got there, I went to climb back in when I noticed something pulling at my arm. Denise was rolling about in her bed giggling, one hand held over her mouth; the other pointing to something behind me, but I didn't take much notice. She had a habit of doing that. Whatever it was tugging at me was really starting to bug me now. I turned around to see which of my tubes had got caught up on something and all I could see was toilet paper...everywhere!

I'd forgotten that I'd got it under my arm. There was a stream of it coming from the bathroom to my bed. How embarrassing! 'I won't fall for that one again,' I thought.

That evening I was awoken by someone gently shaking my shoulder.

"Pommie, Pommie! You've got a visitor...come on now, look lively!"

I opened my eyes to see a middle-aged woman standing at

the foot of my bed. She was a kindly-faced woman, with a strange expression on her face, a mixture of apprehension and pleasure. She started talking as if she knew me.

"...We just flew in a patient...so I asked if I could come and see how you were getting on."

I shifted uneasily in my bed.

"Oh, that's nice."

The woman obviously felt that she knew me well. Oh God... what do I say? I had absolutely no idea who she was.

"You don't remember me, do you? It's okay, this happens, sometimes. The mind blocks out trauma and associated memories. It's the only way it can cope. My name's Edna, Sister Edna."

I smiled courteously and tried to nod in a way that showed I remembered, but I didn't have a clue.

"I was in the aerial ambulance that brought you here. You were in quite a bad way."

I was warming to this lady...but no matter how hard I tried, I couldn't remember her. She continued

"Actually...I popped in to see you about a week ago, and you knew me right away. We had a long chat and laughed about some of the things you'd said on the plane."

I was still drawing a blank. This was embarrassing.

"Please don't feel bad. It has happened to me before. I don't care if you don't know me. I know you and that's all that matters. If it's any consolation, it's a good sign that you can't remember me. The mind is starting to heal itself already. I'm so pleased you're doing well. I'll go now...bye Christina." And that was that. How strange! I thought.

A few days later, Dr Hargrave sat down on my bed,

"So...What are we going to do with you, Christina? Have you decided what you want to do about returning to the Royal National Orthopaedic Hospital?"

"Leaving you will be the hardest thing I have had to do. You know I want to stay here...I don't want to go back. I'm scared of going back to England!"

"I do know...I know more than you give me credit for."

"...but," I continued, "I have such absolute faith in you that I'm going to go...only because you've advised me to...not because I want to."

"There's nothing more I would like more than to keep you here for a few more months, but that would be wrong, when I know your own country has such pioneering work in neurosurgery taking place. Now let's work on getting you patched up well enough for the return journey. I want to keep all the remaining bone intact, but since there's not enough flesh to cover the bone now, we'll have to take the graft from your thigh. We'll take it tomorrow, okay?"

"How big will it be?"

"An eight by six inch graft ought to be adequate...but we may have to go quite deep...we're going to need quite a large amount."

"Will it show?"

What a stupid question, I thought... even as it was tripping off my tongue. What difference did it make now what I looked like?

"It won't be too bad, " he replied.

EIGHTEEN

I began to come to my senses a day or so after the graft had been taken.

Nothing had prepared me for the acute pain one has to endure to get a skin graft. It sent me into a frenzy. Losing an arm wasn't nearly as painful! I thrashed about, tears rolling down my face, in sheer agony. Never again. I kept lifting the bedclothes and glancing down at the eight by six inch patch of nutrient material that had been fused to the open flesh, once the skin had been removed from the thigh. Even when Dr Hargrave did his rounds, there was little I could say. I remember him telling me that, from a surgeon's point of view, I had lovely elastic skin and that they'd put plenty away in the refrigerator to use in the next operation

"We're hoping to get you back into theatre as soon as you are well enough. I'm going to try to get all the grafting done in two operations. You will be pleased to hear that I've taken enough skin for both of these operations – so you won't have to go through that again."

"I wouldn't have done it, anyway," I said, belligerently.

* * *

Everything seemed to be happening so fast now. I was feeling like someone in water, fighting to get to the surface to breathe, but once I'd made it to the surface, my head was being ducked under once more. This didn't just apply to the rapidity of the operations, but also to the fact, ever present in my mind, that I would shortly have to face the thought of leaving this place sometime in the not too distant future. This was something I just didn't want to think about. It petrified me.

I had been in the hospital for several weeks by now. The ward was a bright and airy square-shaped room containing four beds. Along one wall was a large window. I was aware that our ward was on the third floor, so this window would offer a lovely view. However, during the whole time I had been in that room, I hadn't been able to look out of that window. Strange, wasn't it? Not even at the sky.

To me, that window showed the 'outside'. The 'outside' was where I had nearly died. The 'inside', this ward and the doctors, were what had saved me. The 'outside' had tried to kill me. The 'inside' had bathed my wounds and nurtured me. It had become my protection, my womb.

I was loath to face that outside.... ever again.

* * *

Then, one day, I was sitting talking to Peggy. She was in one of her nostalgic moods. Reminiscing about the winding hedgerows that cushion a traveller's way from one ancient Norfolk village to the next.

"I don't know, girl," she said, "I'd be a lot 'appier 'ere if the old country weren't quoit so far away...do you understand what oim siyin?"

She shuffled uncomfortably in her bed. It was difficult to move freely when most of your limbs were chained to a piece of apparatus performing some kind of an unnatural, but essential, task. An old book that she'd been fingering through when I arrived, was lying open on her bed. As she moved to try and escape the sunlight flooding through the window at her side, the book slipped down off her knee and on to the floor.

"Don't worry, Peg, I'll get it," I said, turning around to retrieve the errant volume.

I bent down and picked it up. As I straightened up, I realised that I was now facing the window. I took a sharp intake of air, as the most wondrous sight met my eyes. Panicking, I tried to look away, but the sheer beauty of the view was captivating.

The sea, like a sheet of gently undulating silk, stretched as far as the eye could see. A myriad of the most dazzling aquamarines, emeralds and turquoises shimmered below the cornflower-blue sky. Directly below the window, I could see tropical palms leaning into narrow, curving beaches that appeared to be a sparkling white. Where the sea and the sand met was a ribbon of emerald green. Oh! It was such a sight to behold. As did the wife of Lot...I knew it meant danger...but this was enticing, enchanting. I couldn't turn away.

"You all right dear?"

"Yes, yes, Peg. I – hadn't realised you had such a fine view from your perch," I joked, trying to pull myself away from the view.

NINETEEN

A few days later, I was toying with the idea of making a bathroom visit, when I saw Alfie rushing towards it himself.

'His need looks far greater than mine,' I thought, 'I'll wait a while.'

I picked up my book on Alpha Thinking and read a few chapters. Glancing over to the bathroom, every now and again. The door remained firmly closed with the loud, red 'Occupied' sign showing. Thirty minutes passed and my need was rather more pressing now.

'I suppose I'd better go in search of another bathroom, then,' I concluded

I hadn't yet ventured much farther than the ward, itself, and didn't relish the prospect of doing so now, but there seemed little choice. I shuffled along the corridor, pushing my drip ahead and then catching it up. There was a strange, heavy, musty odour in the air. I tried to speed up, but felt too weak. My shortened arm hung in a sling about my neck.

"G'day!"

I looked ahead, startled. It was the voice of a wrinkled old man, bent and wizened. His skin was the colour of a walnut shell.

"Hello," I made an attempt to sound congenial..

"Oh, so you're *her*...are you?"

"Who?" I asked.

"That woman from England who was rescued by the aborigines out towards the Stuart Highway."

"How did you know?" I asked.

"Papers 'ave been full of it ...and on the T.V. Big news, it is... all over The Territory."

As he made to pass me, a sharp, buzzing pain shot up my short arm. I turned away from him, and it disappeared. Finally, I found the visitors' bathroom by the television room and managed to find blissful relief there. On returning to my bed, I was amazed to see that the bathroom had not yet been vacated. Thank God, I'd decided to seek one further afield.

Having just settled myself back in my bed, about to drop off, I finally heard the door click. To my astonishment, a tall, sultry aboriginal woman walked out, quickly followed by Alfie, who turned to me and flashed the widest possible grin.

"Who was that?" I whispered across to Vera.

"Alfie's wife." came the reply.

"Oh..." I laughed, quietly, "....*now* I see."

* * *

Unfortunately, as my health began to return, so did my appetite. My breakfast generally consisted of toast, accompanied by those airline-type packets containing margarine and *Vegimite*. All this washed down with hot tea.

Lunch was generally a cold dish of some sort. It was always nicely presented, and tropical in nature. But dinner – dinner was wonderful. I always chose the same thing, Barramundi fish. I didn't care how it was prepared. I just loved it, never before having tasted a fish so succulent, yet meaty. Yes, the food was terrific – so, why did I always have this insatiable desire to devour chocolate. Bar after bar of chocolate would wind its weary way through my intestine. Couldn't get enough of it. It was almost as if the accident had blinded me from seeing the consequences of eating so much of the stuff. It became like a drug for me. I had to have my fix of chocolate along with all my other fixes. It was generally bought from the small hospital store, across the road from the ground floor entrance.

On this particular day, I pulled open the drawer of my bedside locker and felt about inside for the familiar rectangular shape of the *Double Deck* Bar. It was a delightful mixture of milk and white chocolate. There was nothing there! I reached up into the corners – nothing. Panic. I looked over at my Mum, who was in quiet conversation with Peggy, whilst giving her a foot-massage.

"Mum, Mum. You know what? I haven't got any chocolate left."

"Yes?" she smiled at Peggy, "what do you want me to do about that?"

"D'you think you could nip down and get me a little bar?" I coaxed.

"Yes, I can do that for you..."

I heaved a sigh of relief and went to settle down for a read.

"...if you come with me..."

I sat bolt upright. The very idea was absurd.

"Don't...don't be daft, Mum. There's no need for both of us to go all the way down to the shop just for one bar of chocolate."

"Both of us can go...or none of us can go...your choice...Dr Hargrave said you ought to do a bit of walking before your next operation."

"Nah.." I said," I've been thinking...I don't really need it, do I? Let's leave it, eh?"

My Mum stood up. She had one of those expressions on her face that I had dreaded as a child. The 'do this, or else' look. My heartbeat accelerated. I knew that this was a lost cause from the start. The bedclothes were flung back and she stood there expectantly.

"Come on," she commanded.

This was my fault. I'd started this. Why did I always get myself into these situations? God, there was nothing I wanted to do less than this. I hated the thought of going too far away from the ward. It took a while for me to get all my equipment to the lift. Mum pressed the call button and we waited. A niggling pounding began deep in my temples. My hands felt sweaty and slippery. The arrow, beside the lift, lit up. We waited for what seemed an eternity. Then, quite suddenly, the bell rang out, piercing the protective silence.

Heartbeat quickened. Sweat broke out on my forehead. The doors opened. There were two or three people already in the lift. Mum and I stepped forward toward the open doors. I faltered, and Mum kept going, firmly holding onto my drip, which, in turn was joined to me – inserted through the neck. Suddenly, I blinked in disbelief as the doors of the lift began to close before my very eyes. Drip in the lift, me outside. Seized by panic. I shrieked at the top of my voice.

" Stop!"

Someone within the lift had the foresight to see what was happening and crashed his fist down on to the emergency button, stopping the lift, just in time. The doors opened serenely, revealing a collection of stunned faces, eyes like saucers, mouths open. By now, I was shaking like a blithering idiot, too stunned to move. Mum grabbed hold of the drip frame and led it and me back into the ward. Not a good first excursion. No chocolate either!

TWENTY

"Pommie, phone call from England."

The nurse's voice echoed down to our ward, from their station, at the other end of the corridor. They didn't even bother to come down and tell me now. I remembered when the first phone calls had come through. Everyone was racing around like headless chickens,

"Oh my God, you're calling from England?"

They'd race down to the ward shrieking, "Pommie, Pommie...phone call from England...quick."

Now it had become a matter of course...

"Yes, Christina Sadler is on the ward (yawn) just a moment..."

I paddled down the corridor.

"How many does this make today?"

I laughed and took the phone that she was offering. The line was crackling, as usual.

"Hello, hello?" I said down the receiver...(pause)

"Tina... is that you? It's Elsie here."

Elsie Mackie was my Head of Department back home in Northallerton...a million light years away.

"Elsie! How lovely to hear from you."

Pause.

"How are you, Tina?"

Pause.

"I'm fine – I'm fine."

Pause. Pause.

"Elsie? Are you still there?"

"I ...I just don't know what to say to you, Tina."

"There's nothing to say...I'm just the same person, Elsie. There's just a little bit less of me, that's all...and that can't be all bad, can it?"

I laughed and felt her relax.

"The kids are all so distraught about what's happened. Some of them had to be sent home from school."

It all seemed so distant – so far away. I found it hard to imagine kids being sent home from school in England because of an incident on the other side of the world.

"They've decided to send you a message on video. They want you to see them. It should be done tomorrow so I'll mail it then...is that okay?"

"That would be wonderful, Elsie – you don't know how good it is to hear your voice."

"Yours, too," came the muffled reply.

"I'd better go now. Remember, we're all thinking of you."

Then she was gone. My link with my old life gone. How would I ever be able to return to that old life, once again?

I replaced the receiver and wandered aimlessly back up to the ward. Another patient passed by on my left. I nodded and smiled. Suddenly, that weird prickly feeling shot up my arm. I wondered what it was; making a mental note to bring it up next time I had one of my *tète á tètes* with Doctor Hargrave.

TWENTY-ONE

A day or so passed and nobody seemed to be bringing me any chocolate. This must be a conspiracy. I yearned to raise the subject of getting a bar of *Double Deck* chocolate from the hospital shop, but knew what that would entail.

Finally, I could take no more. I had to have my chocolate 'fix'.

"Mum," I said, that afternoon, "will you get me a bar of chocolate today?"

I knew what her answer would be before she said it.

"Yes, we can go down now, if you want."

"Okay," I replied. My addiction had superseded my fear.

This time, we made sure to move into the lift with all the drip frames. I'd just had a pain-killing injection, so my mind was clouded anyway. The lift sank to the ground floor. I pushed against the glass doors, trying desperately not to think too much about what I was doing. The hot air punched me in the face as we exited the air-conditioned hospital.

I dully glanced across at the group of aborigines crouching, drips in tow, underneath the casuarinas trees that lined the road leading to the hospital. I could see the store, just across the street. Not far to go now. I felt a kind of sluggish panic as I stood at the side of the road, watching a car drive past. I saw some men dressed in what looked like white overalls, sitting on a seat, soaking up the humid heat. One of them stood up and wandered over in my direction. I thought he was a doctor. As he passed behind me from right to left, I saw out the corner of my eye that he had stopped dead in his track. Something about him unnerved me. Everything was slow and silent, save for the mumbling of the aborigines under the trees. The road now clear, I stepped off the kerb and had just begun to stride across the road when there was a piercing shriek. It came from the man in the white overalls, now homing in on my left arm. His tall, willowy body was hooked over and his highly coloured face was twisted into a menacing expression.

"Ugh!" he exclaimed. "Ugh!"

He came closer still, pointing at my bandaged arm. I reared away from him, trembling and confused. He closed in on me now, shouting at the top of his voice,

"Ugh – What the hell have you done to that?"

He continued to encircle me, pointing. The aborigines fell silent, but nobody dared to make a move.

"You!" he spat. "What the hell have you done to that?"

He pointed, again.

"I had an accident," I said, tears rolling down my face.

My mother hurried me into the shop. The chocolate was purchased and I was led back to the ward, in a dazed state.

'Christ!' I thought. 'If that was how people were going to react to me, I never want to face the outside world again.'

I lay in bed, trying to make sense of what had happened when one of the nurses walked in.

"God! You can't move downstairs..." she moaned, "I had to fight my way through half the patients from Ward One."

"Ward one?" I replied. "What do they do in Ward One?"

"Ward One...you know...the psychiatric ward!"

"Oh," I said, realizing what had happened.

This should have explained away my terror of displaying my arm to the outside world again, but it didn't. Not then, anyway. I had plenty of invitations to go out, but couldn't do it. If someone had told me a few months ago that I would be behaving in this irrational way, I would have laughed in their face. This just wasn't me at all. I'd never had to deal with such feelings before. I couldn't explain it, didn't like it, but could do nothing about it. This fear was real and I was buckling under it.

* * *

Then, one morning, Doctor Hargrave failed to turn up for his morning round. It affected me for the whole day. I missed his cheerful banter and intuitive insights. I wanted to show him how I could now open all those packets of butter and *Vegimite* and spread it on the bread without making a total mess. He always made such a big fuss about everything new that I'd managed to learn.

'Never mind,' I consoled myself, 'I'll show him tomorrow.'

The next day I ate my breakfast so slowly. Trying to save some toast to butter before him, when a nurse came into the ward,

"Christina, Doctor Hargrave has just called. He says he's giving a lecture today and hasn't got time to do his rounds. He needs to see you about your graft operation...so he says you've got to go down to his office."

I looked at her in disbelief.

"What d'you mean...go to his office?" I spluttered, completely taken aback, "He knows I can't walk to his office. It's miles away."

"Don't exaggerate, Christina. It's only a few yards across the lawn behind the shop."

"Anyway..." I went on, racing ahead, "I can't go...I've no clothes. I can't get dressed. I'm in my nightie."

I tried to laugh.

"There's no need for you to get dressed, Christina....just

wear your dressing gown."

"No! I can't do it. I can't go," I said, at a loss for more excuses.

"Well, he says it's do that, or he won't be able to see you until Friday. He's so snowed under with work. It's entirely up to you."

I sat on my bed, festering, with hurt and rejection. He's never treated me like this before. How could he behave so ruthlessly towards me?

I can't go.

I won't go.

* * *

Fifteen minutes later, decked out in a multi-coloured negligèe, a long-suffering mother supported me, pushing my drips along, as we made our way through those hospital doors one more time.

We walked gently and slowly along the winding path, through the hospital lawns. I remember how obsessed I was about trying to miss the water currently being sprinkled all over the lawns to stop them from shrivelling up. The heat pounded down and did little to quell the rage I felt at being treated like this by someone I had come to respect and adore. We finally entered a building and knocked on a door bearing a simple wooden plaque: 'J. Hargrave'.

A middle-aged woman of Germanic origin opened it, promptly. She took my hand, squeezed it gently and smiled.

"Come in, Christina, he's waiting for you."

She led me through another door, into his office. As I entered he had his back towards me and was looking out of the window.

"Where is all this frenetic activity, I have been told

about?"

"Take a seat, Christina," he said, still not facing me.

I sat down, still fuming with anger,

"So what do you wish to talk to me about, then?" I said petulantly.

He swung around on his chair, until he faced me, grinning from ear to ear, "Absolutely nothing at all, my dear."

"What!"

Now I was really angry.

"You brought me all the way over here for nothing?" I was totally incredulous.

"It was the only way I could think of. How else were we to get you to go outside again?"

Suddenly it all became clear to me. This was all a set up. I smiled, but couldn't believe that they had been able to pull the wool over my eyes. I'd been so tied up with my own feelings of rejection and anger that I hadn't thought about the fact that I had walked, quite some distance outside the hospital. Doctor Hargrave saw this as a major step forward.

I saw it as a wicked trick that brought me closer to the moment when I would have to leave for England.

TWENTY-TWO

Finally, the day arrived when I was to have the skin graft put onto my bone. It was with mixed feelings that I faced what was to be the penultimate operation. The closure of the wound would mark the closure of a chapter in my life. Whilst in this state, I was allowed to have weaknesses. I could still have the drugs that I now yearned for, to provide me with a cushion between reality and myself. It was terrific to drift about without a care in the world, but soon I knew I would have to face life without them. Both physically and mentally, they had become my scaffold. I felt ugly and obese, but as long as I had my *Pethadine*, I didn't care.

The wound itself had been open for so long now, that the nerves, left dangling, were doing strange things. It had come to my notice that I could sense, through the end of the arm, when someone was approaching my bed. Powerful thunderbolts of pain would shoot up and down my short arm. It appeared to be perfectly clear to me that, although I had lost the arm, the energy fields around it were still, quite painfully, in existence. This was fun, at first, but by the end of a few weeks, it became a painful annoyance. The operation would, hopefully stop these nerves from this erratic activity. I still had not been allowed to see the stump. This was fine, as far as I was concerned, I did not want to see it in that state. There was no point at all. However, one of the things I would have to do, once it was sealed up, was to look at my arm. I knew that this would have to happen sooner or later... but I much preferred it to be later. Later was coming close now.

Father Tom had just finished praying over me, when the orderly came over to collect me.

"Hello Christina. How goes it?" he chirped, nodding hello to Father Tom.

Everyone down in the operating theatre was becoming quite familiar with me now, since this was my fourth visit.

"See yer later on," he said as he pushed me, on my stretcher, through some swing doors, where the anaesthetists awaited my arrival.

"...You won't see me, though," he chuckled.

* * *

"Just going to take your blood pressure, Christina..."

I opened my eyes and croaked something inaudible at the nurse.

"...you've had the operation...everything went well, just try and get some sleep, now."

I felt completely drained, like a lump of lead in the bed. I usually felt this way if I'd had to have a large blood transfusion, during the operation. I glanced over at my short arm, now swinging in a sling beside my bed and tried to imagine what it was going to look like. Sleep invaded my thoughts before I'd had much time to consider.

"Teen, Teen," something or someone was trying to wake me. I didn't want to know. The noise was persistent.

"Tina, wake up."

The voice wouldn't go away. My right hand was being shaken and tapped now.

God! I thought, this is getting to be really annoying. I half opened one eye and saw my mother's concerned face staring back at me.

"Oh," I croaked, throat still sore from the tubes, "Mum."

I smiled.

"How do you feel, Teen?"

I wasn't yet awake enough to determine how I felt. One thing I did know, though, I needed a drink badly.

"Can I have some water?"

"Yes," she said, holding a cup to my cracked lips.

"What day is it?"

"It's Thursday, love."

"What happened to Tuesday and Wednesday?"

Usually I came round quicker than this.

"You've just been dozing on and off, dear. The nurse has gone to inform Doctor Hargrave that you're awake now. He told me yesterday that the operation had gone really well and that your dressing must not be disturbed for several days. He wants to give the graft a chance to get firmly established."

'Thank God!' I thought.

It looks as if I'll have a few days respite before they haul me off back down to the operating theatre, for my final graft. This was great news. So, I lay there in limbo, as it were, waiting...

* * *

After a couple of days I tried to twitch the muscles in my short arm. It all felt so tight now. It was as if all the fingers of my left hand were scrunched up into a ball and tucked into the end of my arm. I could still feel each separate finger, but it all felt uncomfortably tight. I tried to open the imaginary fist inside my arm, but it sent piercing shooting pains up my arm.

'Best to leave it alone, for now,' I concluded, still yearning to know what it now looked like, but not daring to even imagine.

People kept coming to my bedside with meaningful expressions on their faces.

"Christina, you do realise that, once they remove the dressing, you will only have a stump, don't you? Your arm has gone. You do know that, don't you?"

I couldn't believe that they felt they had to tell me this.

It was as if nobody believed that I'd accepted the fact I'd lost my arm. If only they knew what was really going through my head. I had truly believed, when I was lying on the roadside, with my severed arm lying several feet away from me, that my time was up. I had expected to die, there and then. When I found myself in Darwin Hospital, I was euphoric just to be able to wake up! When you've been that close to death – and you don't die, you couldn't care less which pieces are missing. Just the fact that you're able to wake up is a wondrous miracle. I felt as if I had been given a second chance.

So, the loss of the arm was not the problem. Looking at it for the first time was – but not because I'd lost an arm, but because I was scared at what it was going to look like. I was a class one coward. The last time I'd seen the stump was immediately after it had happened. Bone surrounded by white frilly flesh. I couldn't eat chicken legs for years after the accident! I lay, pondering upon these and other matters, then drifted off.

"Christina," someone was shaking me again.

"Christina, Doctor Hargrave is on his way over to see you, with his team."

He rarely came round with his full team. All systems were go, as I hurriedly ran a comb through my tangled locks and tried to look alert.

It wasn't long before the sound of shoes, clip-clopping along the corridor, and the rustle of starched doctors coats could be heard.

"He's here, Christina," said the nurse, straightening her hair and uniform.

A few seconds later, my bed was surrounded by white jackets. Doctor Hargrave appeared to be in fine fettle, a great big grin on his face.

"Christina...good morning, how are you, my dear?"

"A little groggy, but otherwise good."

"Marvellous, marvellous... Well, everyone, here we have Christina Sadler. When she was flown into this hospital, I truly thought her arm had been chewed off by a croc. In fact, I've told her that's what she's got to tell her pupils when she gets back home..." (ripple of laughter) "Due to prolonged exposure to the sun and insects, it had become badly infected. We have performed three debridements on the stump and have now performed the first of two graft operations to try and close up the wound, so that she can return to England for further nerve-work."

The group all nodded and flipped through my notes.

"I have documented every part of these operations and have numerous slides of the progress of the stump."

My eyes widened. He had taken slides of everything he'd done to the arm!

Ugh!

"Remind me not to come to your house for a dinner and slide show," I said.

"Anyway, now for the great unveiling."

Slowly and gently, he began to remove the bandages from the arm. I looked away, towards my mother, on my right.

"Well," he said after a few moments, "...that's the hard bit over, now we just have to remove the gauze."

I held my breath, but he was working so gently that I could feel nothing at all. I assumed that the stump was fully exposed, on hearing a chorus of exclamations like "Wow" and "Fantastic" and "Tremendous" go up around the bed. Everyone was obviously impressed with his handiwork.

"I don't believe what I'm seeing, Christina," he said to the back of my head, "every piece of skin that I grafted has taken. It's all alive. Unbelievable. I've never had this happen before. You know what this means don't you? There's no need for a second operation. The whole graft has taken. It's a miracle."

I could feel everyone gathering around closer to inspect it.

"What a *great* job, Dr Hargrave. It looks fantastic."

"Christina, don't you want to admire my handiwork, t..?"

"No," I cut in before he had finished speaking "not yet."

"Well, it looks great. I'm thrilled. Now, Sister Egan, there's something I need to talk to you about," he said, walking off, with the group following.

'Wait a minute', I thought. 'He hasn't put the dressing on yet, it's all exposed. He can't just walk away, like this. Oh – I expect he'll return in a second....

But he didn't.

What seemed like minutes passed and I lay there in my bed, frozen into this totally unnatural position, frightened that if I moved, I might accidentally see something.

Everyone had left by now. The minutes ticked on by and my neck began to ache, so I released the pressure a little and allowed my head to fall back into a normal position.

'I'll be okay like this if I keep my eyes closed.'

However, I wondered if I may have caught a brief glimpse of it just before I closed my eyes. Maybe that wasn't it. I'll just make sure of what I saw. I'll blink really fast, just to ascertain that what I saw wasn't my stump.

Blink.

Oh God! It was. It was my stump that I'd accidentally seen and now, through my folly, I'd seen it twice. Just a flash of pink, but that was enough.

Still nobody returned to put on the dressing. I closed my eyes tighter than ever. Another minute ticked by. Maybe I could take a longer peak. If I don't look too long, I'll be okay. I blinked my eyes open and was just about to close them again when something stopped me and I stared.

It wasn't anything like as horrific as I'd imagined. I looked again. It just looked pink. I took a deep breath and let out a long sigh.

"Well, what do you think?"

The sound of a voice made me jump. I glanced up. It was Dr Hargrave standing at the foot of my bed, a great big grin on his face.

"It – it looks all peculiar...sort of...but, not horrible...it looks like a bacon knuckle."

"Well...there's praise indeed!" he laughed.

He squeezed my right hand.

"You're a brave girl."

"You set me up, didn't you? You staged this. Why do I keep falling for your tricks?"

He smiled at me, winked and left.

Alone again, I rolled onto my left side and gazed, intently, at my uncovered arm. It wasn't sadness that I felt, at that precise moment; I was void of all feeling. Before it had been uncovered, I felt a real fear of it. Now I had faced that fear, I felt neither sadness nor happiness. I stared at my arm, mesmerised by it, but completely devoid of any emotion. It was there all right, and I ought to be having some kind of reaction to it, but there was nothing. I felt absolutely nothing.

TWENTY-THREE

"Where d'ya want to sit, dear, beside me or in the back?"

"I'll sit in the back."

I carefully eased my way into the seat behind the taxi driver.

"The doctor said the airport.... International...right?"

"Yes, yes please."

He smiled,

"Get you there in a flash," he said, as he slammed the door of the taxi.

The dull clanking noise it made jarred my sad thoughts. That sound. That awful, final sound. Thank God I'd been pumped full of drugs for the twenty-seven hour flight back to England. I could never have done this, unaided.

Despite the fact that I had my mother there, I felt utterly desolate as the old taxi lurched away from the hospital. I just couldn't believe all this was actually taking place. Glancing back, I tried to smile, waving to all my newfound friends at the hospital. Isn't it strange how close you become to people when you're in hospital? I wonder why that is. I couldn't ponder long upon this matter, as the driver's foot hit the accelerator and we sped out of the hospital grounds.

"My daughter's just recovering from a car accident..." my mother was trying the tactful approach.

"Oh, really, darl," he said, turning his eyes away from the road towards me, "that's really bad news for you."

The taxi was probably just moving along at a regular pace, but for me, it seemed as if we were flying along. Every tiny bump in the road surface sent my jangling nerve ends prickling about my body. You've heard of white heat, well, this was white fear.

After, what seemed like an age, we pulled up outside the airport. I was led into some kind of a lounge, where a group of people that included Margot, Pauline, Peter and Jamie had gathered. I can't remember much at all about this short time, waiting to be put onto the aircraft, but one thing that has always stuck in my mind was a beautiful card from Margot. Inside were the words, "...To the most positive person I know. Love from Margot and Dina."

Apart from one letter almost one year later, that was the last direct contact I was to have with Margot, much to my dismay.

TWENTY-FOUR

The flight home was uneventful. I slept through the greater part of it, waking only to be moved from one plane to another, or to refuel. True to his word, Doctor Hargrave had meticulously completed all the travel arrangements, right down to the taxi awaiting us at our local airport. Well, there's no turning back now, I thought as the white car swept thought the familiar hills and vales of my home country. It was a grey, cloudy day but, despite this, I felt a certain amount of comfort when my eyes fell upon the little patchwork myriad of harvested fields sewn tightly together with prickly hedgerows.

The house seemed so quiet as we entered it, feeling quite strange after the hustle and bustle of the hospital. It smelt different, too – sort of damp or musty. David had built a patio outside the kitchen 'to take his mind off things'. I was impressed. He gave me a long, tight hug, but said nothing. A few minutes later, a neighbour rushed down the path with a large bouquet of flowers for me. It was so surprising to realise how moved people were over the whole affair. I suppose I was fortunate enough to experience people's true feelings towards me without actually having to die. It sounds strange, but that's exactly how I felt. It was as if I had died and, in dying, had broken down all the barriers that usually stop people from speaking from their hearts. The outpouring of love and care was overwhelming. I did not, however, relish the feeling of utter abandonment. Apart from letters and reports – I had no link with those that had cared for me through the worst times. My stump had not yet healed. It needed a considerable amount of surgery before a prosthesis could be fitted. It was now up to me to contact the medical agencies in the UK, and get the ball rolling. I had been told to wait a month before attempting any more surgery, and had been given enough painkillers and antibiotics to do this. All the same, I was terrified at the prospect of putting my medical care into the hands of strangers who knew nothing about what had happened.

I tended to forget, at times, that people at home were not yet used to the fact that I'd lost my arm. I'd had plenty of time to get used to this fact by now and it took a while before it dawned on me that people coming to visit me didn't particularly relish the idea of having to sit and talk normally, as I wandered about with no dressing covering the wound. My brother came in during one of these times, whilst I was allowing the air to get to the stump, and something about the way he reacted, prompted me to inquire;

"Does it bother you, David, seeing this all uncovered?"

He looked up and, for the first time, I saw the pain in his eyes.

"Yes," came his simple reply.

* * *

I had deliberately not informed anyone, other than direct family, of my return - quite rightly assuming that the twenty-seven hour journey would take its toll. It had. However, one morning I got up and decided it was time to face all the kids at school. I made a futile attempt at making my face look presentable, put on a pretty floral jacket and pinned it up so that everyone could immediately see how much of the arm I had lost and called upstairs to my brother.

"David, would you run me to school? I just want to see the kids for a few moments,"

What I really meant was that, I wanted them to see me. If I went into morning assembly, I would get it all over and done with at once. Within minutes, I was being helped into the car and we were off. Pulling up outside the main entrance, the place was deserted. Not a soul in sight.

"Assembly must have begun." I said to David.

He helped me through the front doors and stood in the foyer. The heavy cocktail of school aromas hit me, as I stepped in: polish, disinfectant, kids... I peered through the little round window set in the double doors, leading to the assembly hall. Sure enough there they all were, a sea of emerald green sweaters punctuated here and there by white collars and black trousers. Someone was on the stage reading notices. I was stood there, observing the scene, as if for the first time, through the small round window in the door, when slowly the door was opened and I was beckoned inside. Quietly I tip-toed in and situated myself at the back of the hall. The person on the stage was still talking. A couple of heads turned towards me, followed by a couple more, and more, and more until finally there were five or six hundred heads, all turned facing me. Some were smiling. Some were concerned. Some were inquisitive. The teacher on the stage, oblivious to the fact that he did not have the undivided attention of the pupils, was still reading his notices. I smiled and stood tall for as long as I could, wanting them all to see that I was okay, and that I looked a bit strange. Then I signalled to my brother that I needed to leave and we got back in the car and left.

It was one of those times in life when you are totally over-awed and don't want to comment on it, for fear of it losing its poignancy. Suffice to say that it was one of the greatest tonics I could have had, at that particular time.

Life fell back into a kind of routine. I felt my strength growing each day and looked forward to all the operations being over and done with so that I could start to get on with my life.

One morning, I was in the middle of changing my dressing, when a great big suture popped out of the top of my stump. The revolting piece of black string stood to attention, from the healing mess of the stump. I looked in horror at this foreign body poking out.

'Oh my God, I'm coming undone!' I thought.

I tried to knock it off and then tried to pull it off – but on doing so, sent flashes of excruciating pain up the arm. Sweat broke out on my face as I tried to work out a course of action. Casualty! I need to get down to the casualty department...fast.

I asked somebody to drive me there and was promptly led into a cubicle. Curtains were closed around me. The clock in the ward ticked on. My breath finally slowed down. Several minutes later, the curtain was pushed back and who should walk in, but the doctor I'd seen all those months ago when I'd first hurt my left wrist.

"Now," she said, "Who've we got here?" without looking up at me, she continued, "Christina Sadler...Christina Sadler?"

She stopped in her tracks and, looked up at me.

"Don't I know you? Don't I know that name?"

"Yes, I should think you do," I replied indignantly, "twice I came to see you about a pain in my left wrist and you told me that there was absolutely nothing wrong with it..." I lifted up my stump high in the air towards her, "...now look what's happened!"

Even as the last word tripped off my tongue, I couldn't believe I'd said it. I must admit, I thought it was hilarious to ruffle the feathers of Doctor 'Cool'.

* * *

The episode had been a funny one, but it did start me thinking back over the strange chain of events that had taken place in my life. Had the accident really been an accident, or, as I was now beginning to believe, was I playing out a part in some intricate plot? It began to seem obvious to me that the sudden and mysterious injury that had disabled my left wrist, just months before it had been amputated, had been some kind of preparation for what was to follow. There was no doubt that, once I had actually lost the arm, the fact that I'd already become used to working with one arm, made things much easier. It had become a kind of game for me to find out ways of doing things with one hand. I don't know if I'd have found it quite such challenging fun had I been forced to learn all these things, after the accident, when I was doing it for real, as it were.

After my fourth operation at Darwin, they had sent in the 'Rehab-Nurse' to teach me the basics – such as tearing off toilet paper, brushing one's teeth and buttering bread. She had walked into the ward, weighed down with all her teaching-aids, to be confronted by me changing a pillowcase. This is one of the most difficult tasks we one-handers have to perform. When I related to her the story about the phantom arm injury, she backed out of the ward half-laughing, half in wonder, mumbling, "Well, Christina, I guess you don't really need to be taught any of this stuff."

I smiled at her, a strange but warm feeling coming over me. Had I been prepared? Was someone looking after me? Was this part of my destiny? I started to feel more and more strongly that I could not put all these coincidences down to pure chance. I didn't understand why, but for some reason I was being protected and led in a certain direction.

I suppose it took quite a long while before I fully understood how much of a miracle it was that I *did* survive the
accident. What finally brought it home was when I discussed
the matter with one of the old bush-pilot doctors, who had
worked out in Africa. He was very familiar with my sort of
accident and showed the kind of understanding that only one
who had seen the effect that a harsh, unforgiving landscape
and unyielding heat could have on a trauma victim.

"You don't know how lucky you are," he kept telling me,
"After that length of time, it wouldn't be the loss of blood that
killed you...it's the deep level of shock...yes, I know the shock
saved you initially, by quelling the blood-flow, but you can
only be in that deep level for thirty minutes...an hour at the
most...then it's the shock itself that finishes you off. I don't
know why, but be sure that someone's looking after you."

* * *

One thing could not be denied; there were far too many
coincidences happening to just brush aside the notion that
there was not some higher force at work here. Even the most
sceptical observer could not write off all this as mere good luck.
By now, I knew the truth anyway. These regular occurrences,
which I constantly laughed about, and described as 'weird' to
my friends, were accumulating in number. There was no way
that I could deny that I was being 'helped' in some way.

One afternoon, I was sitting in a lovely relaxed state,
having just listened to a meditation tape, when there came a
knock at the door. I opened it in time to catch Gwyneth Baker
carefully placing her heavy, black steel-framed bike (complete
with basket on the front) against our garage. Now Gwyneth
was no stranger to me. It would be wrong to say that, but I
hadn't seen her for years.

Throughout my childhood, every six months, or so, our family went to the Baker's home for Sunday tea. I'd always been fascinated by Gwyneth – vivacious, strong-minded, interested in absolutely everything. She grew flowers and vegetables, made jams, painted, played the guitar. Her house was an explosion of handicrafts and fascinating books.

David and I always had to be on our best behaviour when we made these visits to the Baker's home. Needless to say, we could never keep this up for long. I recall, on one particularly dreadful occasion, David and I came to blows during a guitar recital by Gwyneth and her two daughters. I still squirm as I see the blood dripping from his nostrils, after I'd packed a punch, and being led by my ear out of the parlour – banished to the car for the rest of the evening.

The memory of that shameful by-gone evening flashed across my mind, as I stood there at our front door, guilt and shame resurrecting itself across my pale face.

Gwyneth, a homely women, short in stature, I would guess in her early fifties, swung round to face me.

"Ah...good...you're in!" she chirped.

She had an interesting face – full lips that fought their way to keep protruding teeth in check and an up-turned nose all drawn together by the most enormous, intuitive blue-eyes. Her shoulder-length brown hair was swept back in a girlish pony-tail. She had the most impish smile. Gwyneth, I know now, was an alternate thinker, long before it became fashionable. She evolved into it alone, instinctively.

"Hello, Tina," she said, "How are you, love?"

"I'm fine," I said, trying not to meet her piercing blue eyes.

I felt sure she could read my very mind. I realised, suddenly, that I was still hovering in the doorway.

"I'm sorry. Please come in," I said standing to one side and allowing her in.

I was still a little ill at ease, not knowing the reason for her visit. She shuffled about in her chair, tucking her voluminous, brightly coloured skirt under her legs. Then she fixed her gaze on me again.

"Tina, I think you need my help."

I was taken aback.

"How familiar are you with alternative medicine?"

"Not very," I replied, warily, "but that doesn't mean I'm against it...just ignorant of it. I know my body has taken a bashing and wouldn't dream of ruling out anything that might aid its recovery."

"Now that's what I wanted to hear. Now I'll ask you again...How are you, Tina?"

Inexplicably, big tears welled up in my eyes.

"Gwyneth, I feel so *tired* all the time and I don't know why. Nothing I do seems to help."

"That's okay. That's normal. It's also normal to shed a few tears. You haven't shed many, have you?"

I shook my head, sending the tears sliding across my cheeks.

"Now, let's get started," she said, laying out, in front of me, a chart full of Latin-sounding names.

Looking back now, it does seem strange that I sat back and let all this happen, without questioning what was going on but something inside told me to let her continue.

"This is my pendulum," she said swinging a piece of crystal in front of me.

"Oh," I replied, stifling an embarrassed giggle.

She proceeded to talk to it. Asking it if I needed any remedies, and if so, which ones and how much of each one.

Gwyneth and the pendulum had an intercourse as follows;

"Does Tina need any Star of Bethlehem?"

The pendulum swung one time.

"It says 'Yes'," she continued, without looking up, "how much Star of Bethlehem does Tina need?"

The pendulum swung twenty eight times.

"Good grief. Are you sure?"

The pendulum swung once.

As she and the pendulum worked their way down the list, I watched with fascination. Either she was an extremely good con artist, or this piece of crystal was moving independently. Gwyneth's fingers were stationary, but the string of the pendulum had a life of it's own. 'This can't be so', I thought. But why on earth would Gwyneth come to my door and offer to do it free of charge, if it were some big hoax? Gwyneth was not the type to play games. She would have been a hard-hearted madam to play these sorts of games with someone in my state, at that particular time. No, this is happening. I felt excited and scared at the same time. How could I ever explain this to my family and friends?

"Have you got a little bottle, Tina?"

"What? Um – yes," I stammered, darting to the kitchen cupboard.

"I'm going to put your remedy into here, with some distilled water and a few drops of brandy."

"Oh," I laughed, trying to act as if this was how I always spent my afternoons, "you trying to get me drunk, Gwyneth?"

She chuckled and after giving me directions, made to leave.

"We've got a lot of trauma to get rid of...I've never come across so much. Take this for a few days...then I'll come back and do some healing," she stopped looked directly into my eyes and added, "If that's what you want?"

"Er, yes, Gwyneth. It's very kind of you to come...are you sure I can't give you any money?"

"No," she said, slipping out of the door and heading for her bike, "I'm just pleased to be able to help."

And then she was gone – leaving me standing in the doorway, trying to make sense of what I had just witnessed.

"If you don't buy a raffle ticket – you can't win a prize," I mumbled to myself, as I closed the door behind me.

With an air of excitement, I darted straight to the kitchen.

"Three drops under the tongue...try to keep it in your mouth for as long as possible...am I going mad...tra...la...la...?"

I did as I had been told and waited. I don't know what I was waiting for but I waited. Nothing. No heavenly apparitions telling me what all this was about. No sudden urges to go and scale Everest. Nothing.

After an hour of waiting, I went upstairs. Maybe it's going to make a visible difference. I stood looking at myself in the mirror. No, there definitely weren't any signs of another hand growing. For God's sake, get a grip on yourself! There are no such things as miracles. You grew out of that when you stopped imagining fairies playing in amongst the flowers on your bedroom curtains. But despite that realisation, I couldn't help feeling bitterly disappointed. What I wasn't clear about was just exactly why was I feeling so disappointed. Was it that I had actually believed a new arm would grow? Or was it that I just had to come to terms with the fact that magic doesn't happen?

I wanted to believe with all my heart that everything that had just taken place was part of some great master plan, gradually unfolding. Accidents don't just happen. Everything has a reason. Surely, I was just grasping at straws? I wanted to explain everything away with down-to-earth, logical reasoning. I really wanted to do this, but no matter how hard I tried, I couldn't shut out those nagging doubts that there was more to this than met the eye. I couldn't explain why I felt the way I did – about everything. Why had I never had a problem with what had happened? Why did I feel that not only that I had been prepared for the blow, but also that, by making the decision to live, I had catapulted myself along a particular life-path? Why had I accepted the loss so easily? Why I had almost been euphoric about the whole thing? Surely, this wasn't a normal reaction?

My mother had put it down to post-trauma euphoria and the heavy-duty drugs that had been administered, but I knew then, and I know now that there had to be more to it than that. I was a whole different person. Now all I had to find out was why.

Admonishing myself for wanting things to happen too soon, I went back downstairs and started preparing dinner.

TWENTY-FIVE

Now, up until that point I had felt that I was doing reasonably well on the 'practical-front'. I decided to try and prepare a spaghetti bolognese for dinner and was busy trying to open a tin of tomatoes with a carving knife when there was a knock on the door. I opened it, and stood face to face with a woman in her late twenties, who introduced herself as the district Occupational Therapist.

She had come, she said, "Just to...talk about how I was getting along."

I bristled immediately, and asked who had sent her? I was doing just fine. Undeterred by my hostile reaction, she invited herself in, saying,

"Well, I've come this far...I may as well have a coffee with you...now I'm here."

I was left standing at the door, open-mouthed, at the audacity of this tiny Scottish lady, with so much gusto.

"I'll go and put the kettle on," I said, expecting her to continue her way into the lounge.

It wasn't until I had actually entered the kitchen, that I realised she'd turned-tail and was following behind me.

By then, it was too late. She was already scanning the disaster zone in the kitchen; a dented can of tomatoes lay on it's side on the draining board, a vicious looking carving knife still hanging out of the jagged tin lid. Tomato juice was splattered all over the surface and tiles, dripping onto the floor. There was nothing I could say. I felt as if I had been caught out.

She took a deep breath and looked me directly in the face.

"Tina, I think we need to talk, before you end up cutting off the other arm," she said, trying to lighten the atmosphere.

It didn't work. I set about making the coffee in silence. I felt extremely threatened and affronted by this woman's very presence, for some reason.

"I'm fine...I can manage. I just have to find different ways to do things...that's all."

She was coming dangerously close to ruining my grasp on everything. Our family had never had anything to do with Social Services. My father had been a Social Worker himself. The thought of actually having to receive any kind of help from them was unacceptable. We had always given help, never had to receive it. I stirred the milk into the coffee and handed it to her, not even bothering to check if she took sugar. I didn't want her concern. I wanted and needed only positive input. Her very presence here meant admitting that there was a problem. At that stage, I couldn't face that. I just wanted people to pat me on the back and say

"I knew you'd be able to handle it, Teen."

So, true to form, up went all my defences. I would have to sit this one out as best I could.

"Look." she was saying, "I know how you feel, Tina, but..."

Now that was the wrong thing to say. Suddenly I saw red.

"How...how *dare* you presume...sitting there with your nice, neat little life and *two arms*...that you...know...how...I... feel. *Nobody* with two arms, who hasn't watched their arm being torn from their body...can have the remotest idea how I feel. *Nobody* with two arms...who hasn't laid bleeding to death in the middle of nowhere, not knowing if they were going to be found in time...could have the *remotest* idea of how I feel..." I was almost spitting these words at her, now.

"I *can* manage, and I *will* manage. Just leave me alone...I

123

just need a little time to work things out...but I can manage. I don't need help from the likes of you."

My words stung. Both she and I knew she hadn't deserved this. She sat there quietly. I bet she'd had to face this sort of an outburst many times. We both knew that it wasn't her I was angry at. She had just been the trigger that had opened a valve and allowed me to vent some of the anger that I hadn't realised existed inside. Once the situation had diffused itself, she came across the room and took my hand.

"We all know you can manage, but Tina, there are so many handicapped-aids I can offer you that will make life easier. I'm sure you have much better things to be doing with your time than trying to peel spuds or open tins without the right equipment. If the technology is there for you, why not use it?" I couldn't answer her.

A river of tears was rolling down my cheeks. Of course, she was right. The problem was mine and it centred around two words *handicap* and *aid*. She'd done her job and knew that there would be no more problems with her 'Client'. She got up and made to leave.

"I'll be back at ten tomorrow morning, if that's okay and we'll talk business – okay?"

"Okay," I said, considerably subdued by now.

She left the house and was getting into her car when I called after her, "Eileen."

She halted and looked up.

"Yes?"

"Thanks."

TWENTY-SIX

There was such an outpouring of concern in the community that, to be honest, I didn't know how to handle it. I loathed going out of the house during times when I would be most likely to meet people. They were always so kind and loving that I felt sorry, in some ways, to have upset them so. My closest friends all handled it in their stride, giving me long hard hugs whilst pressing a good bottle of red wine into my hand.

One day an old school-friend phoned to say she would be coming round to visit me, that afternoon. I perked up and made sure I took an extra dose of my magic remedy - just to be sure of being on form. I wasn't sure how she'd react to me. I certainly couldn't cope if she cried or anything.

Two o'clock on the dot, I saw her walking, brusquely down the drive. I ran to the door and flung it open, standing in the doorway; bandaged arm hanging limply down one side. She glanced up at me, eyed me top to toe, and, smiling said,

"Ooh... yer do look funny, Teen, all lop-sided!"

I loved her for that. We both had a good laugh at what she'd said, and sat down to have a nice cup of coffee. Nothing had changed. The children too, were great – straight to the point.

"What yer dun' to yer arm, Miss? Did all the bone stick out then?"

I continued to take Gwyneth's remedy each day, but to be honest, my initial enthusiasm had waned, somewhat. It was amazing that her pendulum had seemingly come to life, during the session she'd had with me, but no tangible changes were apparent. Or so I thought.

On reflection, I realise now that this was another turning point. Subtle changes were beginning to come about.

I had been in limbo for some time now, not allowing myself to consider the 'what now?' aspect of my life. It had happened. It wasn't half as bad as people imagined. Now I found myself contemplating the fundamental change of character, I seemed to have undergone. For one thing, I knew that the biggest gift I had been given, as a result of all this, was the fact that I now knew that life was finite. This may sound blasé for me to say, but it was something that I had been taught right down at soul level. Most of us imagine that life will go on forever. We all put things off 'until a rainy day' or, 'until we retire'. I was privileged to be shown that life has a beginning *and* an end.

None of us must assume to know when that end will come. Life is so precious and it must be lived in the present. Everything we do, everything we feel, everything we see is precious. Life must not be wasted doing things that don't feel right. There are so many things out there to experience, and from which to learn. We must saturate ourselves with the essence of life and let it mould us into better people, enriched by all it has to offer.

This feeling had always been with me, to some extent, lurking in the depths, but the accident had jolted it to the surface. I now knew that my life-path was about to take a daring new turn. The question was, in which direction?

To some extent, this question was answered almost straight away. A letter arrived in the morning post from Mr Wynn Parry. He was the Consultant, chosen by Dr Hargrave, to complete the nerve and cosmetic work on my arm, prior to a prosthesis being fitted. An appointment had been set up for me to meet him. The limbo had been broken at last. It was now time to move on. I was beside myself with excitement. My doctor had decided that I wasn't up to making the journey by train, so I had to fly. I couldn't wait for the day to arrive.

* * *

Would you take me to the Royal National Orthopaedic Hospital at Stanmore, please," I said to the cab driver.

My flight down to London had been late in arriving in London and I didn't want to miss this appointment. After all, it had been set up on the other side of the World. My arm started to throb a little as we pulled out of Heathrow Airport.

I delved in to the depths of my bag and pulled out my pain-killers. The feel of the small white pill, under my tongue bought comfort, since I knew that the pain would disappear as soon as the edge was taken off my senses by the drug. The taxi drove up and down all the unfamiliar streets of North London, expertly weaving in and out of the traffic. Finally, I noticed a sign with R.N.O.H. on it. At last, we were there. We pulled into the hospital grounds. Stanmore had been an old Royal Air Force Hospital during the War. The whole place looked very forbidding.

"Here we are, love," said the driver, as we pulled up outside the Outpatients Department. "Let me help you out of the cab."

My head was swimming now as a result of the painkiller I'd taken previously, but even so, I could hardly contain my excitement. This was it. This was the place where I was going to meet the man who was going to finally finish all the work on my arm.

Full of trepidation, I paid the driver and wandered in. The clock on the wall showed that I had five minutes to spare – talk about cutting it fine! I was starting to panic. I saw a sign marked 'Enquiries' and went up to let them know that I had arrived.

"Oh, Christina! You made it, then. We weren't sure if you would...coming all that way."

I smiled.

"Come with me I'll show you the way to the waiting room. I was fizzing now in anticipation, and virtually skipped along the corridor beside the nurse.

We swung around the corner,

"Here we are," she pointed to a seat, "You sit there and I'll let Mr Wynn Parry's secretary know that you're here.

I grabbed a seat and sat down. The other people in the room glanced up at me as I did so. I beamed across at them, but, to my astonishment, they just turned away and continued to gaze at the floor. I turned around and saw an old lady sitting along from me. Again, I smiled at her. No response. Silence hung thickly in the neon-lit room. It was a depressive kind of no-hope silence that didn't take long to pull me down off the ceiling and make me feel as flat and depressed as everyone else. Everyone seemed so old. They seemed so full of sadness. I felt a sharp tug at my heart. Was this what it was going to be like? Was this how it was going to be? It was all so negative and alien to what I had encountered in Australia. I became aware of a lump in my throat. I longed to hear some music or some children laughing – anything but this. The only noise in the room was the loud tick of the clock. My spirits dropped lower with every second. Where had all the colour gone from the world? It seemed awfully dark in here.

Finally, after a couple of hours in this atmosphere, a neat little lady appeared, holding a clipboard.

"Christina Sadler?"

I raised my eyes.

"Yes?" I said.

"Would you come this way? Mr Wynn Parry will see you now," she smiled.

'Aha,' I thought, 'smiling isn't out of fashion, then!'

I followed her into an office, where a tall, white-haired gentleman was awaiting my arrival. He stood up as I entered and leant across his desk to shake my hand.

"So, this is the 'outstanding woman of courage' that Doctor Hargrave has written to me about. How is the old fellow?" he asked.

I wasn't sure if he was mocking me or not. He indicated that I should sit down. We chatted at length about the details and nature of the accident and treatment that I'd had in Australia. Finally, he stood up and went to examine my left shoulder. He told me to rotate it.

"Amazing..." he said, finally, in a slightly irritating way, that so many doctors seem to have, forcing you to beg for more information,

"What is?" I obliged.

" Well, I've never come across a patient before, who has had their arm pulled off, and not sustained damage to the shoulder. Are you sure you have suffered no pain in that area?"

"None, whatsoever. That's one of the few areas where I have not had any pain."

"Well, from what I can see, they have done a remarkably good job for you in Australia. All we need to do here is some tidying up and nerve-work. I should think they could have you ready for a prosthesis after two or three operations."

My heart sank. That many!

129

"I'd like to get started as soon as possible. Miss Banks, book Christina in for an operation as soon as is possible. Thank you for coming all this way to see me."

"Yes," I laughed, "you could say that I've come half way around the world. Thank you. Goodbye," I said, closing his office door behind me.

I was duly given a date for the surgery to take place. It was two weeks away. I left the hospital in a taxi, still feeling deflated, despite the meeting. I looked at my clock. It was still quite early. Suddenly I had an idea. I leant forward in my seat.

"Excuse me," I called through the partition, "do you think you could take me to *Harrods*?"

"Sure, love. *Harrods* it is!"

I sat back in my seat.

'A spot of shopping would do me the world of good,' I thought cheerfully, a mischievous grin on my face.

The taxi pulled up outside that shrine to serious shoppers and out I jumped. The door was opened by a uniformed man, wearing an elegant top hat. I started to wander aimlessly through the shop, stopping here and there to feel the texture of a scarf, or run my fingers down a silk tie, quite lost in my own little world, when, suddenly something caused me to look up at the entrance doors.

There, amongst the droves of shoppers, emerged a most elegant looking woman. She was tall, slender and her olive complexion was framed by the most wonderful black hair, all swept up and away from her face in a thick plait. She was wearing a luxurious camel coat and had a stunning, and attentive, male companion.

As she disappeared into the crowd, heading towards the escalator, I tried to carry on with my window shopping, but found I could no longer concentrate. I kept thinking about that woman. There was something about her that was not quite right. I couldn't put my finger on it, but there was something. I kept seeing her image in front of my eyes. What was it? Then, in a flash, it came to me.

She only had one arm.

No, that couldn't be true, I thought. I must be mistaken. But the image kept returning. That was it! She did only have one arm. In a frenzy of emotion, I dashed over to the escalator and couldn't keep myself from walking up it, despite starting to feel weak by now. I alighted at the top and scanned the first floor. She must be here – she must be here. I didn't know why I was reacting like this, but I just had to be sure. I was about to give up and return to my scarves downstairs, when I caught a glimpse of the camel coat disappearing behind a rack of clothes. I darted in and out of the displays until I'd caught up to it. Yes, there she was. Peering through the rows of jackets, rather like something out of the Pink Panther films, I finally got a good view of her.

"My God!" I gasped out loud.

I was right. She did only have one arm. I just couldn't believe it. I had never seen another woman with one arm, before. It was the strangest of feelings. I wanted to leap out at her and say, "Hey! I'm like you, too!" But thank God, I contained myself.

I did, however, continue to shadow the couple around the store, stopping when they did and starting when they did. It was a wonder I wasn't arrested. I was totally in awe of this woman. It probably seems extremely strange to someone who has never lost a limb, but I'm sure there are many amputees who can identify with this episode. The idea of having one arm and still being attractive was not one that had occurred to me. I couldn't believe that you could still consider having a boyfriend or dressing with style.

Finally, after about half an hour of pursuit, I managed to tear myself away from the unsuspecting couple and get a grip on myself again. This had been totally out of character. I have no idea who that lady was and she remained completely unaware of me, but I'm so grateful that she, by her example, showed me that these things were still possible.

The rest of the trip paled into insignificance after my trip around *Harrods*. I bought a couple of bratwurst from the food hall and flew home the following day.

TWENTY-SEVEN

Following my first revision operation in Stanmore, I was informed that it had been a success. Although, I must say, that the impersonal treatment of patients in England was in marked contrast to that which I had been used to in Australia. However, the important thing was that the state of my arm was improving. I was flown back up to Teesside and spent several weeks recuperating.

This time was difficult to get through. Generally, my operation lasted four to six hours, and I would have to be given a blood transfusion. It was no wonder that I felt washed-out. As soon as I got home, I would be bombarded with well-meaning visitors. Children from my school, teachers, cleaning staff, everyone would come around to visit. I had to put on a cheery front for them all and I loved to talk with them but it drained me of every ounce of energy. It became obvious that I needed a longer recuperation period between surgery and visitors. I did not have the heart to stop everyone coming. To do that would have been rude, but something had to be done.

The second operation came and went. My family took the train down to London to visit me following it. Apparently, there had been some problem with my blood pressure in the recovery room and when my family walked into the ward, they were faced with the perturbing sight of me lying unconscious in bed, with the foot of the bed raised high in the air. That was on the Saturday; by the Tuesday, I was told that I could go home. I felt okay, but not quite well enough to do eight hours of entertaining each day (which going home would entail).

What could I do about this?

Then, a thought crept into my mind. When the doctor came round to 'Sign me off', I broached the question,

"Doctor, would it be okay for me to fly?"

"Fly? Fly where?"

Avoiding the answer, I continued, "I mean...is it okay for me to fly with stitches in my arm? Does the arm swell up, like the feet do sometimes, at altitude?"

The doctor, I assume, thought I was talking about flying to Teesside, as I usually did. Thank God, he didn't know that I had not flown down to London, this time. I had taken the train – and would have been taking the train back up North.

"I don't believe so...no...I think you'll be okay flying in a plane."

That was it. As soon as he had left the ward, I was up and heading for the pay phones in the corridor, a pile of pound coins in my hand. I dialled a number and a few seconds later, a voice came on the line,

"Good morning, AFS Travel. How can I help you?"

"I'd like a return ticket to Toronto, please, leaving from Heathrow tomorrow and returning next week."

A few minutes later, I put the phone down, not quite believing how easy it had been. I decided (in my wisdom!) that it would be easier to recuperate in Toronto than at home. There, I would be anonymous. I had to get my stitches out in London the next week, so I would just call back into the hospital after my plane landed at Heathrow. Ordering the ticket was the easy bit. Now came the difficult bit...

"Hello, Mum," I was calling her at work (deliberately, so that she could not make a fuss), "I'm going to tell you something in a moment. Please don't make a fuss...it's all organised now...so nothing can be changed."

"What?"

My Mum sat waiting for the bombshell.

"I'm leaving for Toronto tomorrow, don't make a fuss, I'll be fine. I'm getting a taxi to the airport tomorrow morning and Aunt Hilda is going to pick me up at the other end. I'm fine Mum. If I didn't think that I was up to it, or that this wasn't the best way for me to recuperate, I wouldn't be doing it...you know that."

I could feel her frustration at not being able to argue with me. She sounded frustrated on the other end of the phone and could only say,

"Call me as soon as you get there."

* * *

"You've got all your drugs haven't you, love?"

The sister fussed around me as I put on my thick jacket, manoeuvring it carefully around my bandaged stump. It didn't feel too bad, today. I hoped the stitches would survive the flight. I smiled a secret smile, trying to stay calm, but virtually bursting with excitement. Nobody at the hospital knew what was going on. As far as they were concerned, I was just flying up north.

"Off somewhere nice, love?" said the cabby, after we had been travelling for about ten minutes.

"Toronto," I replied.

"Should be lovely over there this time of the year."

"Yes," I smiled.

" 'Ere we are...KLM check-in, isn't it?"

I paid and picked up my small case and headed for the check in desk. Suddenly I began to feel very weak. A nasty thought occurred to me, 'What if I were too weak to do the crossing?'

I put down my bag. That was the problem. I could walk

okay. It was having to lift the bag that was the problem. I handed my tickets over to the lady at the counter. She glanced up and me and then looked back again.

"Are you okay madam?"

I felt so weak and sick now, that I could no longer hide it.

"I've just had an operation on this," I said lifting up my amputated arm, "I've come straight from the hospital to here."

"Oooh! I'm so sorry. I didn't realise. You shouldn't be walking, let me get you some assistance."

I was too weak to argue. The next moment, I was being pushed along the corridors by a rather indifferent young man. I had to change planes at Amsterdam and the same thing happened. I was transported right to the gate. By now, I was wondering whether had I bitten off more than I could chew.

I caught my reflection in a window as I was being transported to the departure gate. I looked positively ghastly. The people on the desk took one look at me and immediately decided it would be better if they seated me in First Class, where they could keep a close eye on me.

'Yes!' I thought.

The only other time I'd had the pleasure of flying First Class was when I had been flown back from Darwin...and on that occasion I'd been unconscious for most of the flight.

I was boarded and I sank into my comfortable 'armchair'. It was wonderful. There was a leg-rest and it tilted back to a reclining position. Each chair had its own television that pulled out of the armrest. After take-off, I settled into my generous seat and was just dozing off, when a flight attendant tapped me on the shoulder.

"Can I offer you anything to drink, Ma'am?" he asked.

"Yes, please. I'll have a mineral water."

A tray was locked onto my chair and covered by a crisp

white linen tablecloth and a tiny red rose. He proceeded to lay the table with silver cutlery. I was starting to feel very much better. A large dish was then placed in front of me. It was brimming over with fresh salad vegetables, about five different types of fish and prawns scattered around. In the centre of my plate was a spoonful of caviar.

I felt like royalty, savouring each mouthful and delicately sipping my mineral water. When I'd finally finished, I patted the corners of my mouth with my napkin, folded it back into a neat square and placed a hand on my replete stomach.

'A perfect meal,' I sighed, well satisfied.

On cue, the flight attendant leapt into action, clearing away my plate and glass.

"That was delicious."

"I'm pleased that you enjoyed it. Now, can I offer you a choice of dishes for your main course?"

"Main course?" I spluttered, "You mean there's more?"

"Why, of course. You have only had the appetizer!"

"I couldn't eat another morsel."

"Well okay. If you're positive you're done, I'll take away the tray."

"Thank you, so much. You are very kind," I smiled, feeling thoroughly spoilt. "Wake me up when we get there."

I reclined my seat, put my pillow under my stump and blanket over my legs and fell into a deep sleep.

TWENTY-EIGHT

My time in Toronto was perfect. Just what the doctor would have ordered (had he thought of it). I was pampered and massaged and read to. Each day that passed, I felt myself growing stronger. I would get up, languish in a long, relaxing bath, then read for a while and go for a gentle stroll, wrapping up well against the crisp, cold frost outside. The sun shone out of a smooth, azure sky and, as I filled my lungs with the bracing fresh air, I felt that life was just right.

Three days after my arrival, my Aunt came in from work. She sat down with a cup of coffee and said,

"Isn't it dreadful about Kings Cross?"

"What about Kings Cross?" I asked.

"The fire, Tina. The Kings Cross disaster in the tube station."

I hadn't looked at the television or seen a newspaper since I arrived.

"I don't know anything about a fire, Hild, when did it happen?"

"The day you left London, dear, there have been a number of fatalities."

I gasped.

"How awful!"

"Yes. That's why we were so anxious when we picked you up at the airport. I didn't know how you were going to get to Heathrow from the hospital."

"Oh, you needn't have worried about that, Hild. If I had taken the tube it wouldn't have been that line...No...I would only have used that station if I was going to catch the train home to Yorkshire..."

I didn't finish the sentence. We just looked at each other. I had used the train to get down to the hospital for the operation. If I hadn't decided, on an impulse, to go to Toronto, I would have been catching the train North. The train for Northallerton departed from Kings Cross station.

The hairs stood to attention on the back of my neck. It didn't bear thinking about.

* * *

The next day I got up after a long sleep and began to run my bath. My Aunt had such a wonderful array of bath oils. I used to take forever choosing which perfume I was going to try each day. Everything that belonged to her seemed to have that special, 'glamorous' quality. I had always thought, as a child, that she reminded me of Elizabeth Taylor. She had introduced me to make-up. It was my Aunt Hilda who had always discussed the design, or quality of clothes. My Mum had always had the gift of being able to look attractive by just slinging on a dress and running a lipstick over her lips. She had much more practical dress sense. Hilda always smelt of some exotic fragrance as I kissed her cheek. She wore glamorous clothes and make-up. I used to sit and stare in awe as she applied her face in the morning.

I gazed down at the water running into my bath, quickly chose *Lily of the Valley* bath oil and poured it into the bath. Stepping carefully into it, I lay down in the bath. The stump had been covered in a plastic bag because it was not to get wet. Twenty minutes passed by, as I continued to recollect my thoughts on my childhood education from my aunt. Every young girl has an aunt like this. Aunt Hild was mine.

139

Suddenly the sound of the phone ringing shook me out of my reverie. I sat bolt upright in the bath and tried to get out of it as if I'd still got two arms. Immediately I lost my balance and slipped, crashing into the bath, whacking my stump on the edge and sending torrents of water cascading over the side of the bath and gushing out into the landing.

"Oh, no!" I screamed as I watched helplessly.

The bath water gushed over the beautiful wood-panelled floor. My heart was pounding so loud by now I could hear it in my ears. How could this happen? Gingerly, I had a second go at getting out of the bath – this time, rolling over onto my knees (as I should have done the first time). My stump was soaked and throbbing. I was shaking like a leaf. Swiftly, I grabbed hold of some towels and threw them onto the landing, desperately trying to halt the further spread of bath water. I got on my knees with two more towels, and started to mop the deluge. My head was pounding now and I was beginning to feel nauseous. Just as I was wiping up the last of the bath water, the phone rang. It was Hilda.

"Teen, there's something wrong, I know it. What's up?"

She's either got this place under camera surveillance or she's got ESP, I thought...

"I just slipped a little getting out of the bath but I'm okay..."

"I'll be right there."

The phone went dead. I glanced down at my stump. It was soaking wet. I'd better try to change the bandage. I won't go right down to the dressing – that must not be disturbed. I began to unravel the bandage. The arm was still shaking uncontrollably. I took off a couple of layers of bandage and then spotted a drop of blood on the bandage.

'Oh, my God!' I was petrified. 'What have I done now?'

The more bandage I took off, the more blood appeared.

'This is my pay-back for coming here,' I thought.

I had a sinking feeling in the pit of my stomach. I knew that I must not disturb the dressing covering the newly-stitched arm, so I stopped removing the bandage. I didn't want to see what I had done, anyway. A few minutes later, my aunt entered the room only to see me kneeling on the floor, surrounded by a pile of bloodstained bandages.

"Oh, Teen," she said, helping me to my feet and leading me to a chair.

"I think it's best if we don't remove the last bits of the dressing. I don't want to see what's happened. Let's just wrap it up with a fresh bandage."

She gave me a squeeze and started to wind the new bandage around the injured stump, which was still shaking. I popped a painkilling pill under my tongue, although I was not sure if it was to calm the pain in my stump, or to calm me down.

Following that incident, all bathing was done while Hilda was 'in residence'. The rest of the week was wonderful. I was brought cups of tea in bed, along with multiple copies of the *'Enquirer'* magazine. Reading this was quite an experience, especially in my semi-drugged state. I was massaged to sleep with sweetly-perfumed creams and generally spoiled. It was perfect but came to an, all too abrupt, end when I had to leave. I felt like a million dollars as I left them at the airport and boarded the plane back to England.

TWENTY-NINE

Before I knew it, the taxi was pulling up outside the Hospital Out-Patients Department.

"Oh, hello Christina," the friendly receptionist smiled up at me.

"You've come back to get your stitches out, haven't you? I think the doctor wants to examine the stump, as well as remove the stitches. You're his first patient today. Follow me, please."

My heart was pounding so loud. What if I had split it open in Canada? I had to avert my eyes as the dressing was removed. I held my breath.

"Oh," said the doctor...I let out a gasp, "they've done a wonderful job. It's healed up well."

I could have cried with relief.

"You look a lot better than when I last saw you, Christina. Did you have a restful week?"

I beamed up at her.

"Yes, Doctor, you could say...it flew by!"

* * *

Time went by and it was not long before I grew bored with staying at home. Every other week, or so, I had to go down to the London Hospital, to undergo some minor surgery, or have measurements taken, to see if the swelling in the stump had subsided. Then they would be able to start work on a prosthesis.

It was during one such visit that I met Peter. We were both in the same compartment on a train going back into London from the suburbs. He was a handsome man of Polish extraction; we soon struck up a conversation. He was so entertaining. I flirted and laughed for the whole journey. When he announced that the next stop would be his ultimate destination, my heart sank. It had been a long time since I'd had such a good laugh.

He stood up to go, then turned to me and said, "When will you next be in London?"

"Next Thursday, why d'you ask?"

"Well...would you like to go out and do something, Thursday night?"

I giggled girlishly, "I'd love to."

He fumbled in his pocket and pulled out his business card.

"Call me, during the week and we will set up a time and place."

"All right," I grinned, "I'll do that."

It was not until about an hour later that a shocking thought hit me. I had been sitting next to him with my stump hanging away from him out of view. He didn't know that I had only one arm. My mind started doing somersaults. Should I tell him before our date or not? I remember how hurt I was, when a man at our local nightclub had politely backed off, after I had been up front with him about it. Some men are strange creatures. They are so influenced by the physical, rather than the spiritual, side of life. They cannot help but be adversely affected by someone's defects. My mind was made up. I would not tell him until he'd had a chance to get to know me. I would try and make my own fake hand and wear it on the date....

* * *

As soon as I got home, I started onto my brother.

"Dave, d'you think you could make me an arm?"

He stopped what he was doing, and turned around slowly to face me.

"What did you say?"

"I said...do you think you could make me an arm...I'm going on date next Thursday and I want two arms."

"Have you lost your mind, Teen? You can't just 'make' an arm."

"We can. All we need is a bit of wood strapped on here," I pointed to my stump "...and I have a long black evening glove. We can stuff the glove with cotton wool and then nobody will know...see?"

He didn't look convinced.

"Well, let's try it, at least."

"Okay...if that's what you want."

It was obvious that David did not agree with this plan at all.

The arm was ready for its trial run that evening...

Peter met me at Kings Cross railway station. I had on a long, heavy blue trench coat, so the black velvet glove stuffed with cotton wool was hardly visible. Before long, we were laughing our way along the busy roads of London. We decided to go for a meal first, then go to see the newly released film: *Fatal Attraction*. It was showing in Leicester Square and everyone was talking about it. I was very much aware of the 'broomstick appendage' and kept Peter on my right-hand side, whenever possible.

We decided to go to a Chinese restaurant I know in Leicester Square. I made sure I ordered food that could be eaten with a fork or chopsticks because cutting anything up in front of him would be out of the question. Throughout the whole meal, I was so obsessed with trying to act as if I had two arms, that I must have appeared strangely aloof. He kept leaning across the table, gazing at me with his enormous eyes and saying,

"Are you okay? Is everything all right?"

'Relax! Relax!' I told myself, 'You're here, on a wonderful date, with a tall, dark, handsome man and you're in danger of ruining it by being so self-conscious.'

I smiled.

"This is the best Chinese meal I've ever had...and I'm having a wonderful time."

I saw the muscles around his eyes relax, immediately.

"Good," he said, "so am I."

It was a mild night as we made out way out of the restaurant and across the square to the cinema. As we walked along, he took hold of my right hand and swung it to and fro. We purchased our tickets and made our way upstairs to the theatre. The trailers were already showing, and the lights were dimmed as we felt our way along the aisle. Peter halted abruptly at a row of seats about half way up and nodded,

"I can see two seats over there," stepping back, he gestured for me to go first, "...after you, madam," he grinned.

"Why thank you, sir."

I made my way past everyone to my seat. It wasn't until I had sat down that I realised Peter was on my left side, right next to the broomstick handle. Hurriedly, I buried it between my leg and the seat. This was fast becoming a Buster Keaton farce!

The film started. It was captivating, and soon had us all sitting on the edge of our seats and screaming. I had long forgotten the false arm. At one particularly frightening part, Peter reached over and clasped my left hand! I froze.

"Calm down, Tina, it's only a film."

He patted my stuffed evening glove and placed it back on my lap, continuing to gaze at the screen. My jaw dropped and I glanced over at him. Did he or didn't he notice anything untoward about my left hand? He showed no signs of anything being amiss (like a small matter of a left arm!). I found it very difficult to concentrate on the rest of the film, even though it was captivating stuff.

Everyone filed out of the theatre quietly, still shell-shocked I suspect, by the sheer horror, made worse by the apparent reality, of the film. I held my breath. If Peter had noticed my stuffed arm, now was the time he would say.

The chill of the evening air hit us, as we left the building. He took a deep breath clapped his hands together, then, stretching his left arm out, he put it around my shoulders and drew me to him with a big squeeze.

"Phew!" he smiled, quite at ease, "...wasn't that great! It just shows how deceptive women can be!"

I swirled around to face him,

"What do you mean by that?"

"Well, who would have thought that the woman at the start of the movie would have been capable of those atrocities at the end? You women are very adept at concealing stuff from us men."

I stopped dead in my tracks.

"You *know*, don't you?" I said in a hushed voice.

"Know... Know what?"

"Don't give me that...you know, admit it, you know, don't you."

He backed away from me.

"What are you talking about?"

It was obvious, now, that he didn't know anything but I had gone too far not to explain everything.

"Come on. Let's go for a night-cap somewhere and I'll explain everything."

Looking very dubious, he walked along the path in the same direction as me but about a yard away from me. His face was full of consternation. I guess, after seeing a film like Fatal Attraction, he didn't know quite what he was going to hear next. We found a quiet pub on the corner, bought our drinks and sat down.

"Now, tell me what's going on." He was looking angry now.

"You're not married are you?"

I smiled a sad smile and took a deep breath,

"Even if I were married, Peter, which I'm not, you wouldn't be able to tell in the conventional way. You see I have no left hand on which you would look to find a wedding ring."

He laughed nervously,

"Of course you have a left hand, I can see it!"

"No, Peter, what you can see is an evening glove stuffed with cotton wool."

He fell silent.

"Well," he said, after a few moments, "why the big cover-up...why the big mystery?"

"Because I wasn't sure that you would still want to see me, if you knew that I had only one arm."

He fidgeted in his seat.

"Why...why should a thing like that make any difference," he said, but his voice sounded stilted and forced.

At that moment, I knew that I had lost him. We finished our drinks and left the pub in silence. He hailed a cab and asked the driver to take us to my hotel. Looking over at me, he tried to smile but it wasn't very convincing.

"We'll drop you off first, eh? I'd better be getting back home, now...it's already midnight and I have a meeting early in the morning."

"Yeah." I replied, failing not to sound upset.

The cab pulled up outside my hotel and he got up and helped me out. I looked up at him failing to conceal the hurt in my eyes.

"Just tell me one thing, Peter. Did you really not know that I only had one arm?"

"No, I never realised," he replied, "mind you, I did think it felt a bit stiff when I held it in the cinema."

He climbed back into the cab and I waved him goodbye. Well, at least he would have a good story to tell his pals in the pub next Friday night, I thought, cynically.

* * *

Despite that horrendous evening, I used that broomstick handle again once or twice. It had been eight months since I'd lost the arm – longer than that, if you counted the time before the accident, when it had become incapacitated. The first time I had used the 'broom arm', it had felt as if it were dragging on the ground. It really seemed as if it were at least twenty inches longer than the right arm. I was so conscious of this, that I was awkward and clumsy.

THIRTY

I was never to fully regain all the sensation in the stump. The end, where the bone was barely covered by the stretched skin, along with certain parts on the outside, remains numb. Even now, I am forever standing with it on a hot oven ring and won't realise that I am burning it until I smell it. The surgeons in England tidied up all the nerves they could find, by simply stretching them down and clipping them off. However, they could never find the two main nerves, the ulna and median. Their explanation was that, because this was an injury where the limb had been pulled off, the elasticity of the main nerves simply caused them to recoil into the upper part of the arm. I was offered the chance of having these located and blocked-off, as they normally do to amputations, but to be honest, after eight operations, I felt rather like a patchwork quilt. They weren't bothering me at the time, so I jumped at the chance to end further surgery.

I was still getting used to the strange sensations one gets from amputated limbs. Apart from still being able to 'feel', rather than see, someone approaching my left side by the strange tingling feeling that shot up my arm, I can still feel and count on ten digits. When I tell people about this, they usually smile and furrow their brows in a look full of pity, saying,

"Yes, I expect you do still imagine you have ten fingers."

This response always infuriates me, because I don't just 'imagine' that I can move ten fingers. The muscles that moved the fingers are still in existence in the upper part of my arm. Even now, years on, I can still isolate each separate muscle and tell you which finger it moves. I have never lost this ability and wonder if all amputees can do this. If so, why hasn't some boffin been able to harness this energy and invent a *real* prosthesis that can move each finger separately, as they did in their natural state? I know this area is being explored because of the relatively recent introduction of the myo-electric arm, but we still seem to be in the Stone Age as far as all this is concerned. If I had the right background, a scientific mind, I would be so excited at being able to marry our computer progress with some device that could decode and interpret brain messages. I know this must be possible, so what is holding us back? I suspect that it is a combination of lack of money and lack of interest.

Perhaps this area is not glamorous enough to entice those with the know-how and resources away from more appealing issues. I'm sure that if a team of engineers at N.A.S.A. was directed to find a solution to this problem (as part of some space project) they would have it solved in a matter of months. However, that's life, I guess...unfortunately.

Phantom pain is another area that needs to be explored. First of all, I would change the name. The word 'phantom' insinuates that the feeling does not really exist. It does. Believe me, there is nothing imagined about phantom pain. It is very real indeed. It is not always painful, though. Very often, it is merely a sensation – sometimes a very pleasant sensation. I must have fallen out of bed at least four times during the first year, simply because I had woken up from a deep sleep and felt as if my arm was still there. Note that I said felt not thought. The whole arm and hand could still be felt. I would go to sit up in bed, still sleepy, and lean on an arm that no longer existed, in the physical sense, consequently, lose my balance and hurtle out of bed and onto the floor, with a thump.

In time, I learned to recognise this feeling, and am now able to prolong it for a while, by not moving. I can feel everything: wrist, palm, fingers – even knuckles, but as soon as I move, the spell is broken and the feeling disappears. Some days, I get a terribly, itchy palm, or wrist. Other days, I get a painful hangnail or a painful joint in a finger. This sensation is very real, even though the hangnail is not. The only way of getting rid of it is to create a stronger sensation elsewhere, I suppose the brain must dig around and come across some old remembered feeling and throw it out to the senses. I don't know why it happens, but it is very real when it does occur and, usually, if it is not too painful, I love it.

I have stopped trying to convince people of the authenticity of these sensations, because I usually see their eyes cloud over with pity as they pat me on the back and say,

"Yes, Tina, of *course* you think you feel your arm!"

I was so pleased when I read about *Kirlian* photography. Finally, he has been able to photograph energy. I have seen pictures of amputated limbs, showing energy, flowing past the end of the existing part of the limb and forming the rough shape of the lost limb. So, it has now been confirmed. The physical body may realise and see the loss of a limb, but the brain never does, and continues to send electrical messages to those parts no longer in existence. This cannot be disputed. It is now accepted that there appears to be some kind of energy that must be able to exist independently of the physical form. Interesting point to consider – for anyone remotely interested in metaphysics.

* * *

Despite the fact that I could now function well with just one arm, the day loomed when I was going to be ready for a prosthesis. The idea of it thrilled me. The cast was taken and the socket made. Then a colour was chosen (none with freckles to match my own!). A hand was picked (none fitted exactly, but we settled on something between a great big man's hand and a fourteen year old girl's size). All this went away to be assembled into what I was going to call my cosmetic arm.

The process of getting all this together takes so long and involves so many visits that one begins to feel that this is going to take forever. The cost of all these trips to London was starting to build up. I was beginning to get anxious. A school friend of mine, Nicky, called me up. She lived in London.

"Why don't you come and stay with me next time you come down!" she suggested.

I leapt at the chance.

"I'm coming down to collect my cosmetic arm this Thursday," I said.

"Well...come and stay here, we haven't seen each other in ages."

"Great! I'll see you Wednesday evening then."

I put down the phone. It would be great to see Nicky again. She reminded me of much better times. She had been a high-society nanny in London for several years now, so I hadn't had a chance to see her. We would have much to talk about.

Dusk was just beginning to fall as I walked along the lone, straight avenue from the tube station to Nicky's flat. I craned my neck, trying to make out the numbers of the buildings opposite. Then, a waving hand caught my attention. I looked up and there was Nicky waving out of her first floor window.

She had cooked a lovely pasta dish. We sat on the floor, washing it down with wine and listening to music. It was strange, but I hadn't spent an evening like this since the accident. It was so relaxing just to laugh and talk and feel normal again. The years just floated away and we were two wistful young schoolgirls again, taunting and toying with the affections of half the male population in the school.

"So," said Nicky, cheeks flushed and eyes sparkling from the laughter and wine, "what next, Tina? What are you going to do with yourself, when all this is over? It can't be long now before you have your arm completed and you are ready to move on. Anything on the horizon?"

"I don't know, Nicky," I replied, suddenly very serious again, "I need some excitement, a challenge. You know me; I always have liked to be doing something that sets the heart pounding...but what? I mean, look at me! I've put on so much weight. I've lost most of my self-confidence. It's going to be tough finding something that interests me, and that I'm capable of doing, in this condition."

"Oh, you're fine... you'll find something," she said.

That was the beauty of having a friend like her – she never seemed to see or dwell on people's negative traits – dismissing them, with a mere wave of her hand, and concentrating on more 'real' issues. I went to bed that night and slept deeply and well, unaided by painkillers or sleeping drugs. This was a first since the accident. It had done me good to see my friend.

THIRTY-ONE

"Come on, put a little more powder on it and shake it into the prosthesis."

I was now trying to get the finished product on. I hadn't really had a chance to view the prosthesis. It had been pulled out of a plastic bag and was being forced onto my arm.

"It won't fit," I snarled breathlessly at the man trying to help me with the limb.

"It will, it will," he replied patiently, "it has to be a tight fit because it stays on by suction. Come on, let's have another go...there you go!"

He smiled, brushing away the excess talc, "It's on...Go and take a look in the mirror...See what you think."

I turned, walked to the mirror and stood gazing at my reflection. My heart sank. I had waited all these months for this.

"It looks like a Barbie Doll's hand."

"Yes, it is a little smaller than your other one, I agree, but the next size up would have looked like a man's hand...I assure you. There's nothing in between, unfortunately. You can put on a watch and a ring, you know. That always makes it look more realistic..." He carried on talking, but he had lost me.

'So this is it... this is what it is going to be like.'

I gazed down at the shining, plastic arm, hanging, apologetically, down my side. It looked nothing like the real one. I couldn't believe how heavy it was or how long it felt. I would never get used to having such a long arm again. It felt uncomfortable, heavy and alien. I kept looking at it. I couldn't help associating it with things like false teeth, wigs, false nails, false eye lashes. I didn't like any of those and I wasn't going to like this.

"It'll feel strange at first, but you'll get used to it," the man was saying, "Now, you're done with me...but the Doctor wants to examine you, wearing your new arm, before you leave. Take a seat in the waiting room and I'll let them know you're ready."

"Yes, th-thank you."

I was close to tears, as I left his office.

Sitting down, I lifted my false arm up and over, and plonked it into my lap. I felt so depressed. I didn't want to feel this way. I hated feeling this way. It was not natural for me to feel so down. I pretended to wipe my nose with my handkerchief and glanced around the waiting room. There was nobody I recognised. Good. I didn't feel in the mood to talk today. There were a couple of magazines strewn across the coffee table in front of me. One of them was entitled '*British Amputee Sports Association*'. Absentmindedly, I reached out for one and began to turn the pages. Suddenly a headline jumped out at me.

"*Training Weekend with the British Disabled Olympic Team to be held at Stoke-Mandeville. Anyone welcome.*"

I felt as if I'd been struck by a bolt of lightning.

Yes! This was it! This was my rainbow! A goal. A challenge. I had a burning desire to have something ahead of me. It was a way of moving forward. Something positive had to come out of this. I needed to excel at something. *Anything.* I don't know why, but I had to prove that I was still capable of achieving something worthwhile. Going back to my old life was not enough. I wanted to find the reason for it all. Maybe this was it. One thing was certain; I could never have made it to Olympic level when I had been able-bodied. Perhaps this was my chance. I would go to the training weekend. I might be good enough to train for something.

I ripped the page out of the magazine and folded it carefully into my pocket. Meanwhile, Mr Bowler appeared around the corner. My reaction to the arm had obviously affected him. He had his hands in his pockets and coughed awkwardly, before saying,

"The Doctor will see you now."

Spinning around, I leapt out of my seat. He looked up, hardly daring to believe the apparent change in my countenance, as this fireball of energy shot across the room towards him.

"Guess what? I'm going to train with an Olympic team...."

* * *

It was not until the next visit that I could leave the hospital wearing my first cosmetic arm. As I pulled it on, for the final showing to the doctor, it hurt. I couldn't get it to hang right and the tiny hand on the end made the one I had feel even more like the hand of a navvy.

"Walk up there and turn around," said the doctor, nodding up the corridor.

"Okay," I started walking.

"Christina, why are you doing an impression of Quasi Modo?" laughed Dr Marks.

"I'm trying to stop it from falling off!" She laughed again.

"It's held on by suction, Christina. There's no way it'll drop off."

I wasn't at all convinced.

"It feels strange, I know, but you must persevere with it. In time, it will feel much more natural."

I left the hospital, still wearing it. I gazed down at it. It was nice not to see a sleeve flapping in the wind, if nothing else. Feeling clumsy, awkward and extremely self-conscious, I climbed into the awaiting cab.

"Hi!" I smiled over at the driver, "Could you take me to the station, please?"

I fidgeted about the seat, trying to decide where to place my arm. This 'thing' on the end of my arm felt so alien to me that I didn't know where to put it. I had been 'armless' for well over a year, now. It was difficult to think about that arm being a normal length again. It just got in the way and felt clumsy. I found myself thinking that I didn't know how I had ever functioned successfully with two arms of equal length. My little one was much more practical. It never got in the way.

The cab pulled up outside the station. I paid and manoeuvred my plastic arm out of the cab. The station seemed to be buzzing with people and cars. Glancing up at the clock outside, I saw that it was almost five o'clock.

"Great! Rush hour!"

I sighed in dismay, forcing myself into the stream of people going down to the tube. Turning the corner, I noticed that there was a train standing at the station. Everyone pushed and shoved their way on. All the seats had gone, but there was still some space, down the central gangway, for me to stand. I disliked having to do this, because my balance wasn't yet good. The doors closed and the train jerked into action. I held onto the leather handle, for dear life.

The tube stopped every ten minutes or so, and more and more people got on. I found myself tightly sandwiched between an elderly lady behind me, (who appeared to have bought half of Harrods), and a seedy, dark-haired man with a five o'clock shadow. It stopped again and more people squeezed on, pushing me further along the aisle and up against the aforementioned man.

He was now facing me. I looked up at him, an apologetic look on my face. This intimate situation was one, I thought, neither of us could avoid. He smiled back at me, but something about his smile wasn't quite right. Maybe I had imagined it. I looked again. This time, realizing that he wasn't smiling, he was grinning, the widest possible grin.

'Weird fellow,' I thought, trying to move away, but finding myself packed so tightly, it was not possible. I shot another glance up at the man only to find that he was now leering at me in a very familiar way. His grin had, if anything, widened and he was now raising his eyebrows and flashing his eyes at me, whilst nodding his head encouragingly at the same time.

I could hardly believe that this was happening and made one last-ditched attempt to extricate myself from the firm clasp of 'Drooler' and 'Harrods Woman'. I moved slightly, but found that something was stuck, holding me back. I moved again, trying to un-wedge myself, only to discover that what was holding me back was my very own plastic arm. I couldn't believe my eyes. To my absolute horror, my new prosthesis was wedged firmly into the crotch of the Drooler.

Unable to differentiate between the real thing and a lump of plastic, he was standing there giving me the go ahead to continue with, what he considered, a most enjoyable pursuit. Almost collapsing with acute embarrassment, I gave one last heave, and extricated the offending article from the gentleman's thighs. To give him credit, he was as shocked as I on discovering that the cause of so much enjoyment was inanimate!

I must have missed the lesson at the hospital on how to avoid inadvertent fondling on tubes. It was certainly well and truly learnt, now!

THIRTY-TWO

My first job, on arriving home, was to get a letter off to the British Amputee Sports Association asking for details of the Olympic Training Weekend. Shortly afterwards, I was booked to attend the course. This was so exciting for me; to be rubbing shoulders with Olympic athletes. Maybe I would be 'discovered', I mused. Maybe my hidden glories would, at last be revealed, or maybe, as my mother said, I was getting a little carried away.

Me? Get carried away? Never!

* * *

The train pulled into the station where I was going to get off, just as dusk was beginning to fall. I hailed a cab. I was looking forward to seeing the place.

"You visiting a friend, dear?" asked the cabby.

"No," I replied, pumping myself up with self-importance, "actually, I'm taking part in a training-weekend with Olympic athletes, there."

The cabby was suitably impressed.

"So, what sports do you compete in?" he asked.

I flustered a little, but regained my composure enough to reply, "Well, my main event is swimming...and I play a little badminton."

I was trying to sound convincing, but who was I trying to convince, the cabby or myself? I could hear my mother once again, tapping on the kitchen window and shaking her finger at me, whispering, "Tina!" in those admonishing tones.

'Well,' I reasoned, I had been a strong swimmer, when I'd had two arms. I'm bound to stand a good chance against 'disabled swimmers', aren't I?

Shortly after arriving, I was led to a dormitory. It was very Spartan with a highly polished, brown lino floor covering and ten rickety old iron-framed beds lined up along either side. Glancing around, I began to notice that I was, by far, the oldest person in the dorm.

Session one took place in the pool. I bobbed about confidently, as many of the other swimmers were hoisted out of their wheelchairs into the pool.

'Poor things!' I thought, in dismay, as I looked on.

What I had failed to notice was what happened to these people once they were in the pool. Quite suddenly, they became free and mobile, diving and floating about with the best of us. Once we were all in the pool, the senior trainer blew her whistle. Everyone stopped what they were doing and listened.

"I want to do a warm up session, first," she said, her voice resounding across the walls of the pool, "eight laps...any style you wish."

'Okay,' I thought, filling my lungs, 'now that I've learned how to stop myself swimming around in circles...I'll show her what I'm made of.'

She blew her whistle and we all set off. I swam at full-speed, not coming up for air until the middle of the pool. Heaving myself out of the water, I filled my lungs, but didn't submerge again before noticing that the rest of the swimmers had now completed their first length and were on their way back to meet me.

I couldn't believe my eyes. These guys were moving along the water like bullets. I tried to put more effort into my stroke, but to no avail. They lapped me again and again, making me feel as if I were swimming backwards. I'd never witnessed such powerful swimmers. They had finished their debrief and were now well into their training schedule, long before I completed my eight laps of so-called warm-up exercises.

Feeling well and truly humbled, I dragged myself out of the pool, and crept silently back to the dorm.

By the time the afternoon session had come round, I had perked up. I may have been outclassed in the pool, but I still had the badminton session to go. Now, before I lost my arm, I had once been school champion at badminton. I even had a shield on which was engraved:

'Christina Sadler. Badminton Champion.'

'So what, if it had been over twelve years ago,' I coaxed myself, 'you don't forget techniques that win championships.'

I skipped into the gym. There were people in wheelchairs everywhere. I scanned the group for a mobile competitor wanting to have at least one opponent, who stood a fair chance against me. Pride comes before a what?

I felt a tap on my elbow. I looked down to see a handsome face staring up at me.

"Want a game?" he said.

"Er...," I had one last look around for a two-legged opponent,

"Well...okay, then," I said to this bronzed, bearded gentleman.

As we made our way across to one of the far courts, I thought, 'He's far too handsome to turn down. I'll go easy on him. I don't want to deflate his ego. That's the quickest way to lose a man's interest.'

We were now on the court.

"Okay...Let's start by having a knock-around, to warm up, you serve." he said.

'I'll be gentle,' I thought, gently batting the shuttlecock high over the net, and allowing it to drop right in front of my opponent.

Before I could blink, it was ricocheting onto the floor, down to my left. Lucky break! I ran across and picked it up, hitting it gently over the net. Faster than the eye could see, the shuttlecock whizzed by dangerously close to my head.

My partner laughed,

"Just trying to part your hair for you," he quipped.

That was it. War was declared. This guy needed no concessions whatsoever.

I skilfully tapped the shuttlecock into the top left-hand corner of the serving square and centred myself ready to return the shot, covering all angles. It was duly whipped back over onto my side with such speed and ferocity, that all I could do was use my racket as a means of protection. This was all wrong; I was *always* in control on a badminton court.

Here, I wasn't even being given the chance to try any of my strategies. The game started and ended with embarrassing rapidity. I was no match for this man. He was a 'pro' and I was duly thrashed into submission. Totally humiliated, I shook his hand and left the court, praying that I never again underestimate people with disabilities. Apart from the obvious skills, they seem to have this fire in their bellies that lifts them way above most able-bodied people. This gives them the strength to move mountains.

Of course, it was bitterly disappointing to have to face the fact that I did not have what it takes to be an Olympic Champion, but I think the wider lesson learnt here was one that was to carry far more importance in years to come.

I pulled up a seat on the side of the court and flopped down on it. The Olympic badminton coach, saw my face and sidled up to me.

"That was quite a thrashing he gave you, wasn't it?"

I pursed my lips and gazed upward at nothing in particular.

"You saw it then?" I said flatly.

"Yep, I saw it. He's playing extremely well this year."

"Oh," I said, "know him then?"

"Know him? Of course, I know him. Didn't he tell you he's been captain of the Disabled British Badminton team for the past four years."

"No...He forgot to mention that, "I smiled, feeling some-what better, "He plays a superb game."

"Yeah, he's beaten most of the able-bodied team as well...a fine player. So," he went on, "what made you want to come here, on this weekend?"

"I don't know. I need some excitement. I guess. I'm trying to find something that will challenge me...give me some drive. I've always been like this. I sometimes wonder if I'm okay up here," I tapped my head and laughed.

He smiled knowingly.

"Before I lost my arm, I used to do all sorts of crazy things...jumped out of a plane, flew, went sailing...you know...stuff like that. Now that I'm physically unable to partake in those sorts of sports, I'm trying to find something else to do that is equally stimulating. As you may have noticed... it is not proving to be very easy."

"I agree that parachuting on your own would be out...but I'm sure I've heard of disabled people flying."

My eyes lit up.

"Are you sure...where? How?"

" I can't quite remember. I read about somewhere recently

...where was it? Oh...I know! It was in the B.A.S.A. Newsletter. Do you get that?"

"No," I replied.

"Well, you ought to subscribe. The RAF were offering some sort of scholarship to disabled people throughout Britain to go and learn to fly in the States."

By now, bells were going off all over the place. I, too, felt a fire beginning to burn in my belly.

"Where, where can I get hold of this newsletter?" I said breathlessly.

"I think I saw an old back copy on one of the coffee tables in the lounge. I doubt if it'll be the one you want, but there will be a phone number and address. Give them call and see if you're too late..."

I was gone before he'd finished speaking. Hadn't moved so fast all weekend. Sure enough, there was a white magazine, lying on the table in the lounge. I scanned its front cover for an address, but something else caught my eye: *'Flying Scholarships...learn to fly in America.'*

This was the actual issue I needed. I found out where to write for an application form and jotted it down, hardly able to contain myself. The weekend drew rapidly to a conclusion and I soon found myself climbing off the train, again at Northallerton. My brother was there at the station to meet me. I ran up to him, bubbling over with excitement.

"Guess what, Dave, I'm going to go to America and learn to *fly*."

And that was the start of it all. Funny how life works, really!

THIRTY-THREE

Life continued in a relatively normal manner, for a while. I sent off for the Flying Scholarship application and emptied my heart onto the pages. I remember worrying that it was too emotional? Did it seem contrite? I was tempted to throw it away and start again, but something stopped me. I knew that if I wrote the truth, directly from the heart, it would give me my best chance. My application was duly mailed. I recall running around to the little red post-box, the precious package clutched tightly to my chest. I kissed it and then slipped it through the slot, hanging on to it until the very last minute as if trying to impregnate the very molecules of the paper with positive energy. Then, all there was to do was wait. Something I have never been good at.

* * *

The Summer break came to an end and before long, I was standing in front of my new wards, telling them of the wonders they were about to face during their first six weeks in my French class. Most of the children, although new to the school, were already aware of the fact that I had lost my arm. I could see their worried little eyes flitting from my new false arm to my real one, trying to ascertain which one was which. That was one of the sad things about losing my arm. I seemed to lose eye contact, not just with children, but with adults too. Anyway, that day I was proudly wearing the latest technology available to arm amputees, a Myo-Electric arm – an amazing piece of equipment that worked on muscle impulses. If I contracted the little muscles on the upper part of my arm, the sensors would pick up the heat produced and open the fist of the rubber hand by moving the index and middle finger together in one direction, and the thumb would open in the opposite direction, rather like the metal jaws of a clamp. To close the clamp I would just contract the little muscle on the lower part of the arm. The fingers would click into action and slowly move their way to the closed position. Each finger was supported by a frame of solid metal inside. The fingers would only stop moving towards each other once the two metal fingers and the metal thumb had met and could go no further. It was a slow and sometimes painful procedure. I did not have enough strength in my remaining muscles for it to work efficiently, but it was perfect as a form of entertainment at parties. It kept people amused for hours!

There I was, standing in front of the new class of eleven-year olds in a very 'proper' manner. My arms were folded in front of me and a stern but kind expression etched across my face. The children stood behind their chairs waiting for the instruction to sit down. My face broke into a benevolent smile as I continued to welcome them into my class. Then, quite suddenly, I was taken by surprise by the most enormous sneeze. All the muscles in my body contracted together and the Myo-Electric arm started up, moving the metal fingers to the closed position over my right nipple, which, in turn, was flattened between them. I doubled over in anguish and tears started to roll down my cheeks. The pupils shifted about uneasily, looking at one another, eyes as large as saucers and eyebrows raised. They had heard that Miss Sadler could be eccentric, but what was happening here? To them, it must have looked like some ancient ritual or dance. I was in such acute pain that it was difficult, to say the least, to take a breath and contract the necessary muscles to release my flattened nipple. Eventually, I managed to do so, stammering,

"Sit down...you may all sit down...now."

Their eyes still wide and their mouths hung open, as they climbed into their seats, quiet as church mice. Later, I tried to explain to them that my false arm had nipped me, without going into too much detail about the exact location of this catastrophe...

My teaching, at this stage, was most fulfilling. I loved the challenge of teaching pupils who had experienced difficulty in most areas of the curriculum. They usually came to me with that 'I'll never be able to learn French' attitude, and, gradually, I would have the pleasure of immersing them into a new culture. We would learn about French food by eating it. I would play them French music, read them French fairy tales and bring in French cartoons. We would play games to learn the numbers, days of the week and months of the year. We would sample 'escargots', learn to identify various French cheeses, munch on croissants whilst sipping freshly brewed French coffee, and of course, we couldn't forget those frog legs! The one catch was that the only language we could use, whilst in my classroom was French. Together, we learned how to hold simple conversations. I never tired of the rush it gave me to see their little eyes light up as they found they could say something and be understood.

One day, whilst in the middle of a particularly energetic lesson, the French Adviser for North Yorkshire wandered, unannounced, into my room. The whole class froze, in silence, at his presence. Luckily, he saw what had happened and crept to the back of the room, explaining that I had a book he would like to borrow and could he have a look for it in my bookcase. I nodded and swung back around into action. Soon the youngsters were completely lost in their French lesson, the man still rummaging in the corner, long forgotten. After the last of the children had left the room, the Advisor approached me.

"Sorry about barging in on you, Tina; but I'd been told to come and see you at work. That was quite some lesson. Those children were hungry to learn. People find it so hard to get the less-able youngster motivated enough to teach them a foreign language. Those kids were loving every minute of it. I want you to come and give a talk on your methods and techniques to a course I'm running for Modern Language teachers in North Yorkshire. Will you do it? You don't have to give me an answer today, if you wish to think about it first."

I felt that it was a great honour to be asked to do some thing like this, but the very thought of doing it petrified me.

"Yes...I'd love to do it," I found myself saying, "when is the course to be held?"

I couldn't believe that I sounded so eager.

"March 15th," he said, " I believe it is a Monday."

He left the room and I stood there, stunned. How could I possibly carry this off? Give me a room full of children anytime, but adults...fellow teachers! Now *that* was a whole different matter.

I busied myself in preparation for this great event, still six weeks to go. I made a video of my little stars in action; designed games and framed examples of individual pupil's work. The class felt as much part of the talk as I did, proud to be displaying their linguistic skills to all. Soon, well in advance of the great day, my talk was ready. I heaved a sigh of relief. I couldn't have prepared more thoroughly, but this was necessary, because I was absolutely dreading the day with a passion. Now all I had to do was wait...and become more nervous.

THIRTY-FOUR

It felt reassuring to be back into the swing of things. There were times when I hardly dared to believe that I would ever be able to fall back into the life I had led before the accident. I felt so totally changed. Not just physically, but at a much deeper level. I was a different person. I became drained of energy far more rapidly than before. On returning home from work, I usually collapsed upon my bed, falling immediately into a deep sleep. I seemed to be sleeping copiously at that time. On the other hand, I had never felt stronger on a spiritual level. Never before had I felt so in tune with myself. My priorities had been turned upside down and shaken, vigorously, then placed in a totally new order and the newly emerging order, I knew, was the right one for me.

This became evident quite early on in the school term. We all had to stay behind after the end of school for a staff meeting. I was so drained I could hardly sit upright. The question being discussed in groups was exactly how we should correct pupils' work. We were separated into small groups and our group was to agree a policy on how to mark spelling mistakes. I sat there in a detached daze, as the group heatedly discussed whether to underline, circle, or mark the error with a big red cross. I looked on passively, as several of the teachers went purple in the face, their eyes shining with frustration, at what was being discussed. Suddenly, one of them turned to me and said,

"Tina, what do you think we should do?"

I was totally taken aback.

The question had taken me by surprise. How could I

possibly take part in this discussion? At that time, it seemed puerile. I very much wanted to be part of the group and to feel so strongly about the way one marked a child's book, but I just couldn't. The other teachers still had that fire burning in their stomachs. They felt passionately about what they were doing; I no longer felt that way. It was then that I realised just how much I had altered. I had changed – far more than I realised. I felt so confused. Teaching was my life. I still loved working with the children, but I knew that I had gone back to teaching for the wrong reasons. I had returned to prove that I could still do it. For the first time, I felt that I might find life outside the teaching profession more of a challenge. I felt a pang of sadness at this realisation, but knew that it was true and began to wonder how my new life would unfold, but it was early days then.

* * *

It seems amusing now, to think about the way I acted in exasperation, especially where clothes were concerned. If it had buttons, I threw it out. If it had a belt or tie, I burnt it. It never occurred to me that I might become much more dextrous with practice. I just accepted the status quo.

Just before leaving for Australia, I had spent quite a large sum of money on sexy lingerie. I loved to get it out and look at all the pretty lacy bits and the subtle, dusky colours. These wonderful frivolities were now totally redundant. It was impossible for me to fasten all the hooks and eyes with one arm. I tried and tried, but to no avail. I would come frustratingly close to fastening it, then it would ping off and I would be back where I started.

One afternoon, this task became all too tedious and, in a flying rage, I crammed all this beautiful lingerie into a plastic bag and shot off down to a friend's house. I rang the doorbell and when she answered the door, I grabbed hold of a handful of the garments, pulled them out of the bag, saying, "Linda, do you like these?"

"Of course I do, they're beautiful...who wouldn't?" she replied, taken aback at my state of disarray.

"They're all yours...never been worn," I said turning away and jumping back into my car and waving goodbye before she'd had a chance to say anything.

Thank God, I have understanding friends...that's all I can say.

* * *

Following that episode, I systematically went through all my clothes and shoes, discarding anything that had zips, hooks, buttons, press-studs or ties. I pushed them into plastic bin bags and dragged them off down to the Cancer Research shop. They must have thought it was their lucky day because I deposited a great deal of clothing. Now my wardrobe consists solely of clothes and shoes that can be pulled on. No more frustration. I don't need it.

The more I emerged from the sickness of the accident, the more I noticed myself cutting ties and making profound changes in my life. It felt as if I were being led somewhere. I seemed to have little control, nor wanted any. My life, had been whipped up into the air, like a leaf in the wind, and I had no idea which way it was going to blow or where it was going to land.

THIRTY-FIVE

Ever since I had sent off my application form to the Royal
Air Force Benevolent Fund, I had jumped out of bed eagerly
each morning as soon as I heard our mail land on the mat at
the front door. I would race down the stairs and shuffle
through the pile of letters, praying that one would have the
Benevolent Fund insignia on the envelope. I really wanted
this badly. I would sit and visualise myself at the controls of a
little plane, swooping around a blue, blue sky. I had to stop
myself from becoming carried away, and tried to think how I
was going to handle it if I wasn't awarded one. I knew that I
was up against stiff competition. Disabled people from all
over the British Isles would be applying and I was so sure that
mine would be the worst essay that they received.

Time and time again I would collect up all the discarded
letters, having found nothing from the RAF, and stamp,
glumly back upstairs.

Then, one morning, I got up to make the coffee before the
postman had called. I set about preparing the coffee, when a
sudden noise caught me off guard. It was a bundle of mail
hitting the mat. The kettle had just boiled, so I ignored the
noise and finished getting the coffee. Then, when it was done
I sauntered to the front door and gathered the letters off the
floor.

It stood out straight away. The letter had arrived.

Dropping all the others, I shot through to the kitchen,
tearing open the envelope, as I ran. I pulled the stiff white
letter out and held it for a split second, hardly daring to look

inside. My hand shook as I tentatively unfolded the letter. Like lightning, my eyes skimmed over the first line.

"...Dear Christina, it is my pleasure to inform you..."

I threw the letter into the air, not even finishing the first sentence, and ran to the foot of the stairs,

"Mum, I've done it!" I yelled up, "I've got an interview."

A thousand thoughts tumbled around my head, at once. I had scraped through the first stage and had been selected, as one of twenty people, to attend a two and a half day interview. All I had to do was get through this second stage and make it down to the last ten. I scarcely dared think that I might make that far. That fire began to blaze again in my stomach. I was shaking with excitement, and had a grin so wide, it spread from ear to ear. My mum and I danced around with delight.

"Where's the letter, show me the letter." she said to me.

"It's down on the kitchen floor, hang on, I'll fetch it for you."

I raced down the stairs two at a time and retrieved the letter from the floor. I was halfway back up the stairs when I stopped dead in my tracks.

"Oh, no! I don't believe it. They want me to attend the interview."

"Yes, yes I know. That's great, isn't it?"

"The interview is a 2½-day affair that begins at 10 a.m. on Saturday the 13th March. By my calculations, that means it doesn't finish until noon on Monday. How can I be at Grantley Hall to give my talk to the Language teachers of North Yorkshire, when I'm on an interview at Biggin Hill, at least two hundred miles away?"

This was not how I had envisioned it all coming together at all. The school course obviously could not be moved, but

173

maybe there was a chance that I could ask to be interviewed a day earlier....

"No, no. I'm terribly sorry Christina, but an early interview would be out of the question. I would be only too happy to help if I could, but unfortunately, I have already arranged for the panel to gather on Monday morning. Air Chief Vice Marshall Linton and Wing Commander Fielding are flying *especially* to join us on the Monday. I can do one thing for you though. I could see to it that you are first to be interviewed on Monday. That means you'll have to be facing them at eight thirty in the morning, though."

"I'll do it. Thank you so much Wing Commander Pocklington."

So now, I had four hours to cover the two hundred miles from Biggin Hill to Grantley Hall. Could it be done? Well, I was prepared to try and find out.

* * *

Before I knew it, I was climbing onto a train and heading for London, once again. I didn't know why this meant so much to me, but there was no doubting that it did. Was it the challenge? I couldn't clarify it in my own mind. I still felt deep down that I would fail miserably in an interview.

What would flying give me that I hadn't already got? The word sprang forth and almost knocked me over...*self respect.* I knew that this was going to be a tough one...learning to fly...and that was why I was drawn to it like a moth to a flame. I loved a challenge. I needed a challenge such as this, to get me moving again. To where? I didn't know, but this challenge would give me enough momentum to get myself moving along *the path* again.

I pondered upon the last few words my mum had said to me just as I'd left home,

"And don't forget to tell them about your Great Uncle Fred."

"Who on earth is Great Uncle Fred?" I had replied – a bemused expression on my face.

"Oh, haven't I ever told you about Fred? (She knew she hadn't!). Well, as one of *A.V. Roe's* first apprentices, he worked with some of the most well-known pioneers of flight in the country. He was there when Alcock and Brown, in 1919, successfully carried out the first non-stop crossing of the Atlantic. He even helped work on Cody's little biplane, in which he went on to become the first man to fly in Great Britain, in 1908, at Farnborough, Hampshire. Aviation is in your blood, my girl, so go get 'em!"

I had been rendered speechless. My mother's family history had always been something that was simply not discussed. Too many skeletons, I suppose. I had been aware that one of my Uncles had worked, for many years, at the Royal Aircraft Establishment in Farnborough, and that my mother had worked in the tower during the most exciting days of British Aviation in the 1950's, when planes like the *Avro 698*, *Vulcan V-Bomber* and the *De Havilland Comet* Jet-Airliner were being tested. That had been fascinating enough, but Great Uncle Fred! This was something else.

THIRTY-SIX

As my taxi turned into the entrance of Biggin Hill, I drank in the atmosphere of this wonderful old Air Base. On entering my barrack-type accommodation, the air hung heavy with spirits of ancient aviators. I closed my eyes and imagined all those brave young men, with their waxed moustaches, swishing their silk scarves about their necks, as they swept through the corridors forward onto their next mission.

Gradually, the other nineteen interviewees filtered in. There was one wonderful woman from Whitehaven, who had had her whole leg amputated. She was so vibrant and had me captivated with her tales of parachuting and climbing to the top of mountains...on her crutches.

There was also a fellow redhead there. Her name was Linda Hutton. She was the first person I had ever met from Liverpool. She had a warm and caring nature on the one hand and yet, was very down to earth and honest on the other. I felt as if I had known her for years. It was not until sometime after we had met that she finally told me she was suffering from cancer. Not only that, her husband, Brian had been killed in a climbing accident during the previous year. I could have wept. Here was yet another person who had every reason to feel bitter, yet I could see real sorrow in her eyes when she heard how I had lost my arm.

You don't often get to meet people of this calibre in every-day life, but here I was, sitting in a room with nineteen such people – each one a miracle in their own right, bursting with their love of life. They had all, in their own way, seen life at its darkest and yet had sprung forth, in phoenix-type fashion and hit back with double-force. It was humbling to be with these people. They had such positive attitudes and outlooks. I wish I could have bottled the energy in that room.

Here, there were no handicapped people at all. Many of these people had two and three times as much life-force as ordinary able-bodied mortals, lacking in so many of their rich qualities.

The interview and tests were tough. We were given the same entry tests that RAF potential fighter pilots have to undergo. It was exhausting, but also exhilarating. I was buzzing all weekend. Suddenly, before I knew it, I was sitting before the final selection committee. I lost count of the number of 'Sirs' and other titled men on the interview panel. There were about ten, I would guess, all seated behind a large desk, peering at me, a lonely spectacle on a chair, placed in the middle of the floor before them. I think at that point I was beyond plain panic. I was numb. All I kept saying to myself was:

'Just answer everything honestly. Speak directly from the heart. Say what you truly feel not what you think they want to hear...and remember Jonathan!'

Those words ran through my mind like a mantra, over and over again. I was asked about the accident, about why I wanted to fly and why I thought I deserved to win a scholarship any more than anyone else. I replied bluntly that I did not deserve it anymore than anyone else and that was why I felt they needed to find ten more scholarships so that all twenty of us could go to Atlanta to learn to fly. One man asked me why I should be interested in flying when my father had been in the Army. Suddenly my mother's words came back to me. I told them about her working at the Royal Aircraft Establishment during the time of the *Vulcan* and

177

Comet testing. And, of course, I could not forget my Great Uncle Fred, could I?

When I exited the room, a little blue van, engine already running, was ready at the door to transport me at lightning pace to London's Kings Cross station. My head was all of a flurry. I dared not allow myself to ponder on the talk that lay ahead of me. I did, however, give myself the luxury of reflecting on what had just taken place. I knew that I had given it my best shot. I could have done nothing better. I would have changed nothing. I was still so exhilarated, I felt light-headed. The positive energy generated by the group, still bubbled over my every pore.

* * *

As I bounced along in the train, I came to the conclusion that I honestly wouldn't mind if I was not awarded a scholarship. I'd had the privilege of meeting a group of people, the calibre of which, I would be unlikely to meet again in my whole life.

"The next stop will be York station...York station will be the next stop...thank you."

The driver's microphone clicked off and the train drew to a halt. My mind started racing ahead of me again. Try as I might to keep calm, I could not. The thought of what lay ahead froze me with fear. I believe my main problem was that I was not in control of events. I had been forced to rely on other people to make sure all I needed for the talk was placed in my car. I was still having an attack of the "what if?" syndrome, when I caught sight of my sister-in-law, Kim standing on the station platform. I ran over and flung my arms around her,

"Kim, Thank God you're here on time. We've got just less than an hour to get through the York traffic to Grantley Hall."

She grabbed hold of one of my bags.

"We'll do it," she said calmly.

I talked ten to the dozen all the way to the Hall, hoping that my suit was not creasing under me.

Finally, we pulled up outside Grantley Hall. Twenty minutes to spare! We dragged all my lecture aids out of the car and up to the conference room. This was like a nightmare, I thought. I'll never be able to carry this one off. We set up the video and the overhead projector and laid out all the work examples next to the interactive games my classes had made. I just had enough time to run a comb through my hair and apply a fresh coat of lipstick, before the room began to fill up with rather tired and glum-faced teachers. These weekend courses could really take it out of you, especially if you'd had a taxing week (which was generally the case). They all looked as if the last thing they needed, at this particular moment in time, was yet another boring talk. I'd have to do something to brighten them all up.

'Fun!' I thought, 'The only way I'm going to have any impact in this session is to make it fun and...*don't forget Jonathan.*'

So, I did just that. I made them laugh. Combining light anecdotes and a self-deprecating humour with the video and slides, I assured everyone there that was absolutely no need to take notes, since I had brought along a mountain of hand-out material. Instantly, I felt the oppressive atmosphere change to a light amiable one. Before I knew it, my hour was up and everyone was clapping. Relief gushed through me. I don't know if I had done a good job or not, but, as I piled everything back into my box, I felt those embarrassing little tears of relief prickling at the back of my eyes.

Kim, who had spent the hour strolling around the beautiful estate gardens, helped me carry everything back to the car. She looked at me over the roof of the car and laughed.

"You look as if you're going to collapse, Teen. I bet you're really tired. Why does everything you do seem to have to happen at lightning speed?"

"I don't know, Kim," I raised my teary eyes to heaven and smiled, "I just don't know."

THIRTY-SEVEN

The next morning, as soon as I heard the mail drop onto the mat, I lunged down the stairs to pick it up. We had been told that we would not hear about the outcome of the interviews for at least a couple of weeks, but, hey...I had to make sure. Of course, there was nothing, but I always had to check. It was as if I were going to burst with anticipation. I tried to busy myself with other things. My mum had been talking about decorating the kitchen, so, thinking that this would be a great diversion, I asked her if she wanted to go ahead.

She liked the idea, so on our next day off together, we jumped in the car and headed for the wallpaper store. I had been trying to wear my false arm for eight hours a day to get used to it, so I pulled it on and wore a long-sleeved sweatshirt with tightly elasticised cuffs. Unless they looked closely, nobody would have guessed that the arm didn't have warm blood surging through the veins.

We turned in and found a space immediately. Inside the store, there was row upon row of wallpaper – enough to cater for everyone's whims. My mother chose a pattern quite quickly and I began to load the rolls of paper into my arms.

"Here," my mum said, "let me take a few of those rolls."

"No, I'm fine. You just grab hold of the paste, Mum."

As soon as we left the store, I began to feel the weight of the load bearing down onto my false arm. I tried to quicken my pace, but that just made things worse. I could feel my false arm slipping slowly off my stump, but would I admit to anyone that I needed assistance? No! My mother was walking ahead of me, towards the car. The arm continued to slide off my stump. When I stepped off the kerb onto the road, the prosthesis finally slipped off my stump altogether and hit the road with a thud. Luckily, though, the rolls of wallpaper were still balanced, precariously on my little stump.

'Thank God for that,' I whispered under my breath.

Then I looked down. The funniest sight met my eyes. The prosthesis had dropped to the ground, but the tight elasticised cuff was keeping it hanging. As I shuffled across the car park, my arm was dragging along the ground behind me.

"Hey, Mum," I shouted, "Look at this, will you?"

She turned around and started to run towards me.

"No it's all right. I can carry the wallpaper...but don't you think it looks hilarious?"

We both started to shriek with laughter, drawing even more attention to the bizarre scene. By the time we reached the car, our stomachs hurt from laughing and there were tears rolling down our cheeks. As a final lunatic gesture, I grabbed hold of the dangling arm and flung it over the roof of the car, till it hung down the other side of it, still dangling inside the sleeve. It looked like something in a Monty Python film. One poor, unsuspecting fellow almost backed into another car whilst witnessing the whole scene.

* * *

The next day the mail dropped onto the mat and, as usual, I did my now familiar impression of a scalded cat by racing down the stairs. No letter. I didn't think there would be...but you never know. By ten o'clock that morning, the house in utter turmoil as we set about stripping off the old wallpaper.

There came a knock on the back door.

"Just a minute," I shouted, climbing over the chairs and tables to open it.

It was my friend Linda.

Her face dropped, as I squeezed myself out of the back door and stood outside.

"Hi, Lind," I smiled, "we're having great fun here, decorating. Want to come in?"

She peered past me into the shambles inside and shook her head vigorously.

"No, I won't bother, Teen. Actually, I just popped round to drop off your picture."

"Picture?" I asked, "What picture?"

"I'm ashamed to bring it...my mother has taken so long to do it. I bet you've even forgotten that you asked her to do it, haven't you?"

Desperately, I was trying to fathom out what Linda was talking about.

"Come and see it...I think you'll like it."

She had turned and was walking back up our drive towards her car.

"What picture, Lin? What are you talking about?" I yelled, running after her.

I often experienced these kinds of memory lapses, now. The trouble was I didn't know that I had forgotten things until circumstances caused events to resurface in conversation. Linda was now pulling a picture, wrapped up in brown paper and tied with string from her car.

"You'll remember it when you see it...Go on...open it."

Putting it on the car, I undid the string and folded back the brown paper to reveal a beautiful arrangement of pressed flowers. There were all sorts of small flowers: Daisies,

Buttercups, Bluebells, Pansies, but the most predominant and pretty flowers in the arrangement were the wonderful sprays of Forget-me-nots. I let out a sigh, but no words would come, as I remembered all those ions ago, giving Mary Meynell, Linda's mum, a box full of pressed flowers to arrange in a picture. Linda was one of the few people who realised the significance of these flowers. Finally, I swallowed and shook my head.

"Linda, tell your mum it's more beautiful than I could ever have imagined. Tell her I will treasure it."

She wrapped it up and handed it to me.

"I know," was all she said, then climbed into her car and drove away, leaving me clutching the picture to my chest.

Not wanting to bump into my mum, I went back into the house through the front door and climbed the stairs to my bedroom. There, I lay the picture on the bed and stared at it once again...

* * *

The memory of a hot summer's day came flooding back. My father was lying on the thick green lawn of our back garden. It must have been some time in June, because the entire garden was filled with a dazzling display of flowers. My mother had painstakingly planted them all in the spring. They were now in their full glory. I sat some way away, staring at him. Even though it couldn't have been more than two or three months before he lost his ultimate battle against cancer, he was still a picture of health and vitality. How I loved him!

We had known he was dying for several months by then, but it didn't seem real. Our dad was invincible, or so we had thought. I had just discovered a little flower-press in the attic, and was busy trying my hand at pressing some of the blooms from the garden. The flowers made me happy. Their beautiful, perfect simplicity brings out a hint of purity from even the hardest of hearts. Sitting there, picking out the ones that were going to go into my press, watching my father doze in the sun, I could almost, for a brief moment, have forgotten the painful reality of that time. My father stirred, as a little plane flew across the clear blue sky. We both followed its progress as it looped and danced across the sky. With considerable effort, he raised his head off the grass, looked over at me and smiled.

"It must be wonderful up there today," he'd said, then slowly settled his head back down into his lush pillow, crossed one foot over the other and spread his arms out on the lawn, as if he, himself, were that soaring plane. A smile spread itself across his face as he fell back into a deep sleep.

Somehow, I knew then that when I reopened the flower-press, he would no longer be with us, but at least I would have preserved this precious little memory in these dried flowers. I closed up the press, wound down the butterfly clips and lay down on the lawn, too, lost in the dance of the little plane, darting about in the summer's sky. Were we looking up into the future?

I would like to think so...

Memories are such wondrous gifts, overflowing with joy and sorrow at the same time. I dried my eyes, took some deep breaths and carried the picture downstairs.

THIRTY-EIGHT

The next five days passed. The mail came and as usual. I leaped out of bed to retrieve it. My nerves were jangling by now. I had been in phone contact with several of the other applicants and they were the same. The waiting was unbearable. I started to mull over all the things I had said, during the interview, trying to think how I could have said them in a better way.

By the end of the first week, I had managed to convince myself that I did not stand a chance. There was no way I stood any hope of winning a scholarship. Once I had resigned myself to that fact, I was okay. Well, at least I could function relatively normally for a few hours anyway.

Then, on the ninth day, the letter finally arrived. I swiped it off the carpet and raced through into the kitchen, tearing it open as I went. I hardly dared read its contents. My eyes skimmed over the first sentence:

"Dear Christina, I am delighted to inform you..."

I could scarcely breathe, let alone believe what my eyes were telling me. I was beside myself with sheer joy.

"Mum!" I bellowed up the stairs in as loud a voice as I could muster, "Mum, I've done it. I've been awarded a scholarship."

Even though I was mouthing these words, I could hardly take in what I was saying. I felt as if fireworks were being fired off all around me.

"That's great news, love," she said, hugging me at the bottom of the stairs.

It was great news. In fact, it was the best news I'd had in a long, long time. A short while later my newly found friend, the one-legged chiropodist from Whitehaven called.

"Have you had your letter yet, then?" she said.

I knew by the flat tone in her voice that she had not been as fortunate as I.

"No, Anne, I haven't got mine yet," I lied, "why...have you got yours?"

I didn't want to make her feel even worse by telling her that I had been successful, because I knew she should have gone, instead of me.

"Yes," she replied, "I was rejected, wasn't I?" she said miserably, "I expect they thought I was too old or something."

I couldn't believe that she hadn't got through. She was an ideal candidate – Vivacious, intelligent, adventurous, with a quiet determination that I had rarely seen in a woman. She had told me the story of how she had parachuted, piggy-back style from a plane after she had lost her leg at the hip. She had also climbed one of the highest peaks in the Lake District...on crutches. Her eyes had glistened with pride as she had proudly described how her hands had been torn to shreds, by blisters, but she had done it – on one leg. I was so sad that she would not be coming to Atlanta.

Later on in the day I heard from Sandra Sutton. She had been asked to try again next year. They didn't feel that she was emotionally ready to face the rigours of the flight programme yet, since her husband's death had not been that long ago. She, too, sounded so flat and disappointed. I continued to pretend that I hadn't heard yet. I was losing my effervescence rapidly now. All the candidates who had seemed obvious choices had not been selected. I was beginning to wonder what criteria they were using to select.

I perked up when my brother came around that evening and we cracked open a bottle of champagne. It heartened my soul to see how pleased my family were for me.

* * *

The following three months passed by with a flurry of preparations and learning. I went to work, but found it difficult to keep my mind on school life when, there, just over the horizon, lay a little *Cherokee Warrior* PA 28/161, anxiously awaiting my arrival in the Deep South. Oh! It all sounded so exotic and exciting. I was counting the seconds as they ticked on by.

Finally, not a moment too soon, the day came when I was to leave Northallerton and head south to Gatwick Airport. My mother and I had decided to make the trip together, enjoying a few days in the Reigate area, where my father had grown up, on the way down to the airport. It was a strange thing for my mother to suggest, but my knowledge of father's childhood days was extremely sketchy to say the least, so I was pleased to go along with it.

His childhood, if you can call it that, left a lot to be desired. Dorothy May was just fifteen when she gave birth to Antony Frank Sadler. It was rumoured that his father was a gentleman from Belgium. Baby Antony was promptly dispatched to her adoptive parents. His 'adoptive' grandparents were gentle, kindly folk who did what they could but they were advancing in years.

At the tender age of seven, he found his grandmother dead in the garden. He pulled the body inside and ran to the newly installed telephone, fathomed out how to use this mysterious contraption and finally was able to get the sad news over to his grandfather.

I never knew his mother. For all I know she could still be around. I was told that she spent her life moving from man to man and country to country. Over the years, I ascertained that she had been an extremely beautiful woman, in a dark sultry sort of way. How or why I came to this conclusion is unclear, since there was never a photograph of Dorothy May in our family home. I also gleaned that despite her lowly start in life, she was highly intelligent. She managed several pubs in the centre of London; sailed off to South Africa with another man to set up a fish and chip shop; she also worked in the household of Ernest Jones in this grand old country house named 'The Plait'.

Ernest Jones was one of Sigmund Freud's first 'disciples' in England. In 1938, following the Nazi occupation of Vienna, Freud sought refuge with Jones in 'The Plait'.

It was during this time that there came a twinge from the maternal side of her soul and Dorothy May sent for her son Tony. My father vividly recalled one day, sitting on Freud's knee in the mansion gardens. All he could say about this momentous occasion was that Freud was "...a very old man with a snowy white beard." Freud died the following year.

The interesting thing about this is that he never mentioned any of this to me. He rarely said anything about his childhood. What had prompted him to tell me then was that he had caught me researching in one of Ernest Jones' books for a paper that I was writing for my teaching degree.

* * *

We decided to stay in Reigate because my father's grandfather had once been chief gardener in the Castle Gardens in Reigate. The rose garden he had designed and planted still existed and we wanted to see it.

It was an odd time, really. We had fun together, we always do, but it was as if we were clutching at straws. Trying, in our way, to find my father in his past since we had lost him in our present. We found the rose garden. It was beautiful and the air hung heavy with pungent perfumes. I could see my father, as a young boy, ducking amongst the bushes. My mother told me tales of his Grandfather, Frank Sadler, who, though unrelated by blood, had perhaps had the most profound influence on my father during his formative years. It all seemed so distant though. My father had spoken so little about his past, this man just seemed like a kind stranger. We searched in vain for the graves of his grandparents and finally left Reigate for Gatwick Airport after two days, having made little headway.

I was sad to say goodbye to my mother, but it was only for six weeks, and this was too much of an adventure to be downcast for long.

* * *

I was a member of a group of four scholarship winners, two girls and two boys. The other girl, Jane Cross, was a pretty girl with the most vibrant red hair, I believe I have ever seen. She was busily trying to say farewell to all her family, when I arrived. She looked pale and strained, almost fragile, as she sat with an austere expression on her face, in her wheelchair supervising the loading of her luggage.

Whereas Jane appeared to be about my age, the boys, Stuart and David, were both considerably younger. Stuart came from the West Midlands. He had dressed in a smart suit for the flight, cream in colour, a dramatic contrast to his jet-black bristle-cut hair. He wore glasses that seemed constantly to slip down his nose and he walked with abject pain and difficulty, using crutches. His poor wasted legs dragged along behind him as he went. He had spinabifida and so had to live with this testing condition throughout his whole life. He looked over and saw me looking, a smile spread across his pensive face. He was obviously thrilled to be going to Atlanta, but did not want too many people to know it.

David, too, was in a wheelchair. He had a pleasant face, rounded with chubby little cheeks. He spoke beautifully, with an endearing lisp. He dressed in a bottle green polo-necked sweater and black denim jeans. He was in deep conversation with Wing-Commander Pocklington, the man who headed the scheme.

So, after bidding our fond farewells to our loved ones, we were led through to a lounge and offered cocktails. All four of us were buzzing with excitement, but didn't want to show it. We all wore fixed smiles on our faces as we secretly sized each other up.

The flight was a rather long and sticky affair. Arriving eight hours later, looking rather worse for the flight, we were met by Bill Langtry and Richard Wilton (two flight instructors from Epps Flight School), along with Don Morgan. Don had been present at our interviews in Biggin Hill. It was very reassuring to see his familiar face I can tell you.

After we had retrieved our luggage, we were taken to Bill's mini-bus. My first impression of Atlanta was that of a hot, sticky, cloying place. We all ate and then retired early to our rooms at the motel. The next day was orientation. I couldn't wait to see the planes. I wondered who would be my instructor.

* * *

It was obvious from the outset that we were going to be treated just the same as anyone else coming for flying lessons. No allowances were going to be made because of our disabilities. This fact frustrated us somewhat initially, but eventually made what we achieved more meaningful, because we knew that, although it had been a struggle, we had done it on our own without any concessions having been made.

The instructor who had drawn the short straw and been allocated me as a student was Rob Compton. He turned out to be a mild-mannered 'gentle' man from South Carolina in his late thirties. At the time, he and his wife were managing to bring up a wonderful family of two boys and three girls on the meagre wage paid to flight instructors. Rob's dream was to become a Missionary Pilot in a Third World country. His life was tough and he had to fight hard to keep his family fed, but he was overflowing with spiritual goodness. He was so poor, materialistically, but everyone who came in contact with him could not miss the riches he had discovered, spiritually. He lifted everyone he met onto a higher plane, both physically and spiritually. His joy was contagious, somehow.

My introductory flight was to Gainesville, Georgia. I bolted my flying 'piece' onto the yoke, merely to test if it would fit. Obviously, I wouldn't be doing any flying on this my inaugural flight. I sat back and relaxed into my seat for what, I had presumed would be a sightseeing tour to familiarise myself with the aerial view of the vicinity. Little did I know how wrong I was. No time was wasted in handing over to me control of the plane. I was mortified, as I stared blankly at all the moving dials in front of me, striving but failing, to remember what each one meant. Then, to add to the confusion, a voice came over the radio.

"Blah blah 47 Yankee...blah ...12 o'clock...blah blah!"

192

A microphone was thrust into my hand.

"Just say traffic sighted...47 Yankee," said an amused instructor.

I did as I was told and began to feel I had bitten off slightly more than I could chew. There was no way I was ever going to be able to interpret all the data being shown to me on these instruments.

Once we had returned to Peachtree-Dekalb Airport, I was both alarmed and bewildered. I climbed into the back of the station-wagon that had been sent for the group. It was driven by a bare-footed man with a couple of day's growth covering his chin, who chewed consistently on a straw. I grew to love big-hearted Emory, our noble chauffeur, who had been given the dubious honour of transporting us to and from the flight school.

The other group members also seemed to be subdued, I noticed on the way home. Nobody spoke about their flights at all. This was certainly a different crew here than those who had boarded the plane at Gatwick.

There, we had been pumped up, by all the media coverage. We had each been built-up into local celebrities at home in England. Here, all that meant nothing. Here, we were merely students in the art of flying.

This flight today was our first go at getting hands-on control of a plane. The complexity of it blew one's mind. There seemed to be thousands of pieces of information that one had to interpret and assimilate in order to leave this 'earthly place'. I knew I wasn't an idiot, but maybe, this time, there was a chance that I would not be able to succeed. A cold feeling crept from the base of my neck, down my spine and settled in the pit of my stomach. It was an uneasy, tight feeling. It was the feeling of imminent failure. I had never thought of failing before. What if, after all this hype, I couldn't do it? How would I ever be able to face my family and all my pupils after failing?

I stared out of the window of the cab. Suddenly, Atlanta didn't seem half as glamorous, as it had when we first arrived. It was a heavy, humid day with low clouds that made everything touched seem hot and sticky. The busy six-lane highways appeared cheap and tacky with all the signs and bill-boards nailed to posts at the edge of the roads. All the buildings were square and functional. No money had been squandered on the aesthetic quality of anything. I now ached for the elegant, soaring edifices of Paris. I ached for some culture. I felt so alien here, starved of beauty – or so I thought.

I ate my dinner in the restaurant and went to bed, feeling very despondent indeed.

THIRTY-NINE

The next day I was awoken by a chink of light forcing its way between my heavy, hotel curtains and dancing over my face. I felt well rested; my mind had now shaken off most of its jet lag. On pulling back the curtains, it was as if someone had been out with their paintbrush all night, sprucing up the world. The sky was a clear, vivid blue, the like of which I had never seen before. The leaves on the trees were so green and perfect they looked unreal. Everything was alive today, visibly pulsing with vitality.

On arriving at the flight school, I was amazed to find that even that place didn't look as dingy and depressing as it had on the previous day. We were warmly welcomed by the Chief Dispatcher and office manager, Kathleen. It was her job to schedule us all in the correct planes. Paraplegics in the group were limited to using the two adapted *Warriors* of 822OH or 8445B (since these had been adapted for wheelchair access and had hand-controls fitted). I had to have a plane that was a stable flyer and did not have a stiff yoke, since my false arm could not take a lot of unnecessary stress.

After the first few lessons, we were allowed to pre-flight the plane on our own. I used to love this part, since I felt it was a way of getting to know the plane and all its own individual foibles. Each plane had a character all of its own. They may seem similar at first, but anyone who flies know this not to be the case. I loved to lift up the engine cowling and peep over the top at the engine.

As a child, I had never been encouraged to get involved with the mechanical side of things and so the opportunity to get real grease on my hands, as I felt along the pipes and cables and checked the oil and brake-fluid, was a rare treat. As our ground school lessons progressed, so did our knowledge of the aircraft itself, and what made it fly. I had the added bonus of having an Airframe and Powerplant Mechanic as an instructor, so he was able to go into this side of it in greater detail.

Yes. Learning about what makes a plane fly whilst on the ground was one thing. However, getting up there and putting it into practice was an entirely different concept. The truth of the matter was that, although it had been almost three years since I had lost my arm in the car accident, I was still very much ill-at-ease when travelling in anything that was moving fast, be it cars or planes. I always began to hyperventilate. Sweat would begin to accumulate on my upper lip and temples. This was soon painfully obvious to Rob, my instructor. Taking off and flying around was fine. The problem became apparent when we came into land.

* * *

Many people have asked me what was more difficult: taking-off or landing? There is no question that landing requires, by far, the most skill. A plane is built aerodynamically. It wants to fly. So, unless something very unusual goes wrong, it is relatively easy to get a plane airborne. Landing is a different matter. As soon as I turned final during those early lessons, my heart would go into over-drive and I would have a full-blown panic-attack on my hands. Rob would look over at me, and his face would become ashen as he decided just how far he was prepared let me mess up a landing, before taking over the controls and rescuing us from the hands of death.

Those final moments before landing inevitably consisted of me, trying to curl myself up in a tight ball, with my one free hand clenched tightly over both eyes, emitting a shrill, high-pitched scream as loud as I could. I can make a lot of noise at the best of times, but imagine having to suffer that kind of noise within the confines of the cockpit of a small plane.

Every time we went up, I would promise Rob, faithfully, that I would not do it and, time and time again, I broke down and found myself doing it.

While everyone else in the group would be discussing the new manoeuvres they had mastered during that day's lesson, all I could do was remember the anguished screams that accompanied my every landing. I was so busy rolling up in a ball and covering my eyes that I hadn't even tried to land the plane. Then, after one particularly harrowing lesson, Rob sat me down on a chair in his office.

"Tina," he said earnestly, "do you want to fly a plane or not?"

I looked at his face and my heart sank. He looked totally exasperated.

"You know I want to fly, why do you ask?"

"Well, we can't go on like this. Unless you can overcome this fear you have, we may as well give up now. I have done everything I know to help you get through this and nothing has worked. You are just putting both of us at risk each time we land, and beside that, we are wasting time and money."

I felt totally crestfallen. Of course, he was perfectly correct.

"There is only one person who can help you overcome this thing...and that's you yourself. Think about what I have said today. I know you can do it and I want you to do it...but only you can decide if you are going to do it."

He left the room and I sat there, my eyes raised towards the ceiling, fighting the tears that were pricking the back of my eyes. The sad thing was that I couldn't dispute a word he had said. The only person that could get me over this paranoid fear of seeing the land come swishing up towards me, at 70 knots, was Christina Sadler. Yes, I did have every justification for feeling frightened, but that did not mean that I had to give in to it. A decision had to be made. Was I going to let this fear overcome me, or was I going to fight back? Once I had thought about it in these terms, there was no question what the answer would be. I went back to the hotel and slept deeply, promising myself that I was going to show Rob my first controlled landing the very next day.

Flight training at PDK Airport

FORTY

As soon as my alarm went off, I jumped out of bed and set about gathering all the flying equipment needed for the day. I had been given a piece of equipment made out of metal that had been used by a one-armed pilot. It consisted of a universal socket that had a bolt on the end of it, which I locked onto the yoke. It looked awful. I loathed getting ready to fly and having to click this ugly piece of steel onto the end of my appendage. I always left it until the last minute before attaching it.

The clear blue sky beckoned, surreptitiously, as I went out to pre-flight the plane. It was only ten thirty in the morning, but just a few minutes into the pre-flight, I was dripping with sweat. I finished off the oil-check, closed the right cowling and opened the left cowling. As I lifted it up and peered inside, I saw a great big bunch of keys lying along the top of the rocker arms. That cunning instructor of mine was checking that I was carrying out a thorough pre-flight. I smiled to myself, picked up the bunch of keys, slid them into my pocket and went on to complete my pre-flight.

By the time Rod appeared, I was sitting inside the cockpit, firmly bolted to the yoke. Rob double-checked the plane, then jumped up onto the wing.

"Ready?" he said, grinning from ear to ear.

"Yes, I'm ready, Rob," I replied without so much as a mention of a certain bunch of keys found lurking in my little engine.

He climbed inside and fastened his seat belt and shoulder harness, still glancing over at me with an expectant grin on his face. I didn't falter but continued with my internal pre-flight.

"Er..." he coughed nervously, "Tina...did you notice anything unusual during your pre-flight?"

"Now, it's funny you should mention that, there *was* something," I said completing the last few parts of the checklist before starting up the engine. Rob heaved a sigh of relief.

"What was that, then?"

"Well, I noticed that one of the tie-downs was badly in need of repair..." I said, as I completed the final pre-ignition checks and lent forward taking the keys between thumb and forefinger, as if I were going to turn it.

"Stop!" he shouted, lurching across the cockpit and snatching my hand away from the ignition key, "Don't start it!" he bellowed at me.

"Why ever not, Rob?"

"Didn't you see anything unusual in the engine today?" He was looking annoyed now as he started to unbuckle himself from the seat in order to retrieve the keys himself.

"What? Oh...d'you mean these things you 'accidentally' left on the rocker arms?" I said coyly, throwing them into the air so that they landed in his lap.

"Gotcha going a bit then, didn't I?" I laughed, as I pulled open the storm window and yelled out behind "Clear prop!" for the second time before starting the engine. I love double-bluffing people...such fun.

Once we were airborne, I lost myself in concentration and was unable to worry about the fast approaching landing, but, as with all good lessons, they come to an end and I could feel the atmosphere change abruptly as we called up Tower to inform them that we were heading back in from the north-east Practice area.

Everything went to plan. I found myself turning final for runway two-zero-right. I expect Rob was tensing up every muscle in his body at that point, preparing for the usual histrionics. I took a deep breath and instead of watching the ground rushing up, fixed my gaze on a point further up the runway that wasn't moving so fast. It worked, and, although the usual panic wasn't gone altogether, it had subsided considerably. I didn't cover my eyes or scream the place down. Well – okay – there was a slight whimper, as I flared too soon and the plane fell out of the sky, doing kangaroo leaps up the rest of the runway before coming to rest in its own parking space outside Epps Flight School. It had been a messy landing by anyone's standards, but Rob was ecstatic.

"You didn't scream! Good work, Tina. That was great, in fact. You did it at last...I knew you would...Now all we have to do is to teach you how to land a plane without damaging the landing gear!" He laughed.

To any onlooker, it would have been described as the worst landing ever but, to us, it was a major break-through. I had overcome what had seemed an insurmountable obstacle between myself and the chance of being able to fly a plane. After a couple of celebratory drinks with Jane at the hotel bar, I went to bed, convinced I had now pressed the fast forward button as far as my flight training was concerned. Little did I know...

FORTY-ONE

Several lessons followed, during which various different types of contraptions were strapped onto my short arm for me to test. Not one of them gave me the ability to control the plane solely with my left arm, which was what was needed for a landing. Every time we came in, I smacked the plane down. Rob usually had to test the ELT, pump up the wheel struts or send it into maintenance for the nose-wheel to be checked.

It was not only acutely embarrassing, it was also frustrating. Everything was being done by trial and error (mostly error, in my case). There was no way I could progress along this flight-training course until something could be found that could be used to land the plane. Solo-ing was out of the question, until I had proved I could fly and land the plane safely, without help. This could not be guaranteed with the selection of flying aids that I had been given so far. It seemed now, that there was no way through this latest obstacle.

Two people in our group had already solo-ed and were confidently continuing their fight programme. I felt so sad and frustrated all the time. I enjoyed the theoretical side of the training, finding it exhilarating to go back to the books and study after years of teaching.

Now that it was the middle of summer, the temperature would shoot up into the nineties on the airfield by about 10.45 in the morning, when we would be starting our pre-flights and. by the time we finished and sat inside the cockpit ready for the lesson, the thermometer inside would be registering one hundred and ten degrees. I gave up wearing any kind of make-up because it always ended up running down my cheeks. The pre-flight would be followed by an hour's lesson, which in turn, was followed by a fifteen-minute de-briefing session. Despite Rob's attempts to find something positive to say about my flying, by the end of the day I felt totally and utterly demoralised and drained of every ounce of energy.

I now had twenty-three hours of flight and fifty take-offs and landings (that were anything but normal). It was possible for someone to pass their whole Private Pilot's Licence, with just thirty-five hours of flight on a Federal Aviation Authority approved syllabus. Here was I, clocking up the hours like a slot machine in Vegas and I couldn't even get the plane down on the runway. The, now customary, taxi-ride back to our hotel was worse than usual. We all sat there, dripping with sweat, craning our necks to catch a little cool air from the inadequate air-conditioner in the cab. I was crestfallen, hot and frustrated. I turned to Jane (whom I suspect had just had a wonderful lesson, but was sensitive enough not to tell me) and blurted out,

"What the hell am I doing here, Jane? I'm just wasting everyone's time and money."

I was on the verge of packing it all in and returning to less foreign parts. I felt so low, such an utter failure. Even the other three members of the group were progressing at a steady pace, despite their numerous handicaps. I, on the other hand, hadn't managed to make an ounce of headway – and we had been in Atlanta for twenty-two days, now. What had made things worse was the fact that I had heard rumours about Rob, my flight instructor, being severely reprimanded by his superiors because of my apparent lack of progress. The fault was not his at all. He had been the most patient, inspirational instructor possible. He had never tired of trying to teach me the basic manoeuvres over and over again. The fault was mine. Was I just plain stupid? Had the accident and the drugs affected my brain? Why, when I had memorised all my procedures, and carried them out meticulously, could I not grease the plane onto the runway, the way I'd seen so many other pilots do from the observation deck in front of the Tower?

"I'm going for a swim in the pool when we get back," Jane said, "Why don't you join me?"

The cool clear water of the pool sounded very appealing at that particular moment.

"Yes – I think I will."

Jane had already swum two or three lengths by the time I'd managed to locate my swimsuit and changed. She loved the freedom that being in the water gave her. She looked up and waved as she spied me waddling along the side of the pool. As I slid my hot body into the water, I let out a long, slow sigh. It felt so good to be cool once more with the sun lying low in the sky. I swam a couple of lengths but tired quickly, so just turned over and floated on my back. A few minutes passed where my mind was freed of turmoil and I was allowed to lose myself in 'nothingness'. Then, just as I began to enjoy my tranquillity, wisps of my present reality began to creep back into my consciousness. I swam a couple more lengths, hoping that the exercise would help me return to my peaceful place, but this time it did nothing but agitate. I clung onto the side of the pool and began some leg-stretching exercises. What on earth was I going to do? Jane swam up to me.

"You okay?" she said.

"Not really," I replied flatly.

She seemed so full of confidence about her flying. I knew she absolutely loved every minute of the new-found freedom that flying had brought into her life. That's how I should have been feeling, but I wasn't. I hated it all. It had made me feel angry, frustrated, stupid and a failure. But all that was nothing was compared to the shame I felt at letting my instructor down

"Just pray, Tina, pray," he had urged me, "God is with you just ask for his help."

"Huh!" I thought, bleakly.

I just couldn't understand why everyone else could do this thing and I could not. The only difference between me and the rest of the group was that they all had both hands

Jane smiled compassionately,

"You know, Tina, when we arrived here, they had already found something for us to use within the plane that would do everything that our legs could not. They had a tried and tested piece of equipment, the hand-control to work the rudders. They have not yet found a piece of equipment for you to use that will do the job of your left hand. They're still working on it; you are bound to lag behind until they have fixed you up with something suitable. Don't give up, now."

Jane was normally such a private person, these words she spoke now seemed to have so much more of an impact.

"Yes...I know you are right," I smiled, unconvincingly.

* * *

Later that night, I lay in bed trying to shake a pounding headache. The pressure, both internal and external, was tremendous.

'I don't need this kind of pressure so soon after my accident,' I thought, saturated with self-pity.

The bed in which I was lying was all untucked and dishevelled now. Through my twisting and turning, I had flung my nightdress on the floor because I was so hot and sticky. All I wanted to do was sleep. The more I worried, the less chance I had of getting the rest I needed to be alert and fresh for the next day's lesson. I glanced over at the digital clock on my locker...two fifty-seven. What on earth was I to do? I had to be up and dressed in three and a half hours. I turned over, pumped up my pillow for the twentieth time and flopped my head back down into it.

"Please help me," I woefully cried, up to the heavens.

Then, taking a long, slow breath, I closed my eyes, falling into a deep, restful sleep. Peace had descended, at last. I was flying. Flying in circles with a beautiful white seagull.

* * *

Awaking just hours later, I was surprised at how refreshed I felt, although I was still functioning like a robot. Collecting the keys, I went out to pre-flight. Despite feeling more refreshed than I had in a long time, I was dreading yet another unpleasant experience in the air and that sinking feeling gripped my stomach, as I did the final checks on my walk-round. Here I was, talking myself into another dreadful lesson. The weather didn't help either. It was a cloudy, grey day and there had been a little drizzle earlier. I climbed across into the left seat and bolted the knitting needle contraption onto the yoke, then opened up my chart to study whilst I awaited Rob. Several minutes later, as he climbed into the right seat, his customary infectious smile spread across his face and his eyes shone with enthusiasm. He belted himself in, then lent across and took my chart out of my hand, throwing it into the back seat.

"What are you doing? I *need* that!" I snapped.

"No you don't, Ma'am. Today you an' me's gonna have some fun..." he clapped his hands together. "Come on...Miss

Tina, let's go on an' get us up there!" I started her up and off we went.

"Six – six – golf – cleared for take off two zero right – six – six – golf."

I released the brakes and gently pushed the throttle forward.

"Geronimooo!" howled Rob as we sped down the runway.

Just as we were lifting off the ground, a beam of sunlight forced its way between the clouds. It was still drizzling a little. We tracked the zero four zero radial away from the airport to the North East practice area. Once there, Rob took the controls and began to swoop and dance all over the sky. I found myself laughing and giggling like a schoolgirl.

Suddenly, I looked ahead and saw the most beautiful rainbow shedding a myriad of brilliant hues before us. There is no sight more pure than that of a vivid rainbow. Man could never spoil that fan of iridescent beams. I marvelled. It was still raining up there, even though the sun shone brightly now, turning each tiny raindrop into a minute prism that filtered out all the different colours composing white light.

"Look, Rob...just look at that! Isn't that just the most beautiful sight...let's get closer."

He glanced across at me, pleased at my response to the vision.

"It's your airplane, Miss Tina," he said, relinquishing the controls.

I swung the plane around and headed straight for it.

"Hey!" Rob said, "We can practice our Turns about a Point, round it, can't we?"

"Yes," I answered, "that'll be great."

I was so at ease now – it felt good. After a few minutes of flying in circles, I became puzzled. Try as I might, I couldn't get near to the end of the rainbow. I grew anxious.

"We don't seem to be getting any closer, Rob, it almost seems to be moving as I approach it."

He looked incredulous and burst into laughter.

"Of course it's moving...it's refracted light, Tina. You can't catch it up...but you know that, really...don't you?" he patted me on the shoulder," I always knew you were a rainbow chaser! It sure is good to chase rainbows...don't you think?"

I laughed at my folly.

"You may find you cannot reach the end of the rainbow...but I'll show you what you *can* do, though," he said pointing to the middle of the arc, "turn the plane and head under the middle of the arc. Hit your dream head-on, as it were!"

"Is this another game, Rob?" I grinned, quite happy to play along.

"Just do it," he quipped, faking exasperation.

So I did. After a few seconds, he took hold of the controls.

"It's my airplane – now take a look out of the side window."

I turned my head to the left and looked up. I could still see the rainbow...but much closer.

"Now look down, look down, Tina."

I looked and gasped. The rainbow was now a complete circle, going right around the plane. I looked up again, hardly believing what I was seeing, and followed the spectrum of incandescent coloured light that was now encircling our plane. It was an incredible natural wonder. *We were actually flying through a rainbow.* I leapt about with sheer joy, inside the cockpit.

"Amazing, truly amazing! Do it again, Rob...do it again."

"It's your airplane, Miss Tina. You are Pilot in Command. If you want to fly through rainbows...do it, girl! Go, do it!"

I checked the airspace around, and behind, the airplane.

"Clear!" I confirmed.

Then I swung the plane over into a perfectly controlled steep turn and headed back towards the rainbow. Luckily, the sun was still out and I did it again.

"Boy! Were we flying now?"

The beauty and purity of the experience took my breath away. I climbed, then descended, carving deep arcs into the sky. It was intoxicating.

"Just watch out for that bird over there. You wouldn't want that to hit your window, believe me."

He pointed to a white bird in the distance.

"Oh, I will Rob," I said, scrutinizing his face to see if the white bird in the distance held any significance for him. He kept looking ahead of him. I returned to my flying.

Rob Compton – My Flight Instructor

Half an hour later, still playing in the sky, lost in concentration, Rob tapped me on the shoulder.

"Time to get the current weather information from ATIS and call up the tower," he said.

The hour's lesson seemed to have flown by.

"Do we have to? I want to stay up here forever."

"'fraid we do," he replied with a smile.

His plan had worked. He had rekindled that little flame, just when it had been in danger of going out....

"Tell you what, I'll even help you land the plane today...don't want to ruin a great lesson," he smiled!

It hadn't been just a lesson to me, and he knew it. I had been given a taste of the celestial beauty, awaiting me. At last, everything seemed clear to me. This was why I had wanted to fly. Now all I needed were the right tools with which to do it. I was being educated on many levels.

FORTY-TWO

That night, just as I was putting away my study books in my room, there came what seemed like an explosion. The walls of my room shook and the lights went on, then off, then on. I peered warily outside through the curtain, but jumped back sharply as there came a second explosion even louder than the first. I was shaking now, checked that my door was firmly bolted and climbed back into bed to read. Then – crash – a third explosion shook the whole room. The lights flashed on and off, then on, then off. The television went dead. Silence ensued. This was scary. I fumbled for the phone in the darkness and dialled Jane's number. She was in the next room. She picked up.

"You okay?" I whispered.

"Yes..." she stammered, "...what's going on?"

"I've no idea, but stay in your room. Is your door locked?"

"Yes, but what's that noise outside our doors?"

I held the phone away from my ear and listened. It was a slow pit pat sound – maybe it was some kind of animal.

"I'm going to take a look, Jane. Don't hang up...I'll put the phone down on the bed and have a look."

The pit pat sound seemed to be speeding up. I slid off my big bed and crept across the floor to the door. The noise was louder. I could hardly breathe. I placed my hand on the door-knob and opened it. Suddenly, there was a blinding flash of light outside. It was eleven o'clock at night and yet it looked like the middle of day. A large heavy drop of rain plopped down my nose, followed by several more, then came that thumping explosive noise, again, rattling the window panes.

Before the echoes had died away, the heavens opened as if someone had opened a million faucets. You could almost cut through the energy in the air that night. I scrambled back across the room to the phone.

"Jane – you still there?

"What's going on?" she cried.

"Get in your chair and come to my room...you don't want to miss this. It's a thunderstorm to end all thunderstorms. I've never seen anything like it. When the lightning strikes, it's like broad daylight outside. Come and see!"

A few seconds later, she appeared outside my door, holding a video camera.

"I want to record this – they'll never believe it at home, otherwise," she said.

Each time the thunder clapped, the noise was deafening. I had never before witnessed such unbridled, natural energy. We laughed excitedly, gazing out upon the whole scene with a sense of awe and sheer wonder. One cannot help but respect a power that can conjure up energy such as this. I had only ever come across anything like this one time before. That was the night my father died.

Eventually, we gave in to our sheer exhaustion and retired to our beds. The sound of the pelting rain and thunder filling our ears.

The following day, it all seemed like a dream. The sky was blue; the sun was shining, the humidity was low and a cool, light breeze was blowing.

As soon as we reached the flight school, Richard Middleton was standing there waiting. He thrust my flying-arm in front of me.

"I took this home last night, to try out an idea I had. See how you get on with this, today," he said triumphantly. I looked down at it. He had dispensed with the precarious universal socket joint, put the original hand back on the arm and reinforced it by wrapping sheet metal around the whole hand and wrist. Before, I had always had to bolt myself onto the yoke.

"How do I keep hold of the yoke?" I asked intrigued by this new turn of events.

"Aha...well...I've made up this strap that wraps around the wrist and hand. You simply strap yourself onto the yoke now. I held it together with *Velcro* – but you may well need a buckle before we're finished."

Thrilled by the fact that someone seemed to be making a positive move to solve my problem, I pulled on the false arm. It felt like a lead weight – but at least it still felt like an arm. This thing had real possibilities. I already knew how to use an arm...I wouldn't have to learn a whole new range of arm motions to manoeuvre this piece of equipment. I couldn't wait to try it out.

"Which plane am I, Kathy?"

"Eight – four – six – six golf," she replied with a smile. I felt a new lease of energy.

"Perfect! My favourite plane!"

I grabbed the keys, fuel-checker and checklist and headed out towards my plane, passing Jane sitting in her wheelchair in the hallway.

"Good luck," she grinned.

* * *

The new arm felt good. It felt like an arm should feel. Anyone watching me from the observation-deck would never have guessed that one of my arms was false. A thick black leather glove hid the reinforced steel. I sat in the plane, studying my procedures, whilst I awaited my instructor. It was not long before I looked up and saw him coming out to the plane. He climbed in, big smile on his face and said,

"Well, now, Miss Sadler, why don't we go give this new arm a few tests?"

"Okay!" I laughed, "Let's do it!"

"After you've given me my full passenger briefing, I want you to call the tower and advise them that we're headin' on over to Charlie Brown airport...a workout on runway niner over there, ought to put the new arm through its paces."

We departed the pattern and headed over to Charlie Brown Airport - a short, narrow runway carved into a densely wooded area. There was little room for error here. It was easily hidden by trees, even on downwind. I knew my landing procedures by heart. I recited all my power and flap settings in my sleep. Turning onto final approach, I hesitantly let go of the yoke with my right hand and placed it back on the throttle. This was when things usually started to go wrong. The preceding arms that I had attempted to use didn't seem able to control the plane on its own. I used it to turn the plane into the wind. It worked. It actually worked.

"Now...keep your right hand on the throttle until I tell you otherwise."

I held my breath, felt for the wind and continued to ease the plane down with my false arm.

"Trim, Tina, trim!" Rob was shouting "You don't have to take the full load of the plane on that arm."

I did as I was told. About two hundred feet off the ground a gust of wind blew the plane momentarily off course. My right hand leapt automatically towards the yoke.

"No!" shouted Rob, "Keep it on the throttle...feel your way down...pitch and power...pitch and power...come *on* now."

The little plane eased itself onto the runway, with the grace of a swan. My eyes were out on sticks. My jaw dropped open. I turned, with a look of astonishment and glee, to Rob.

"Rob, Rob...I...I..."

"Drop you flaps and apply full power...we're doing it again!" he yelled above the roar of the engine.

Not one of the eleven landings I went to do that day was as pretty as that first for me, but at least I was bringing the plane down with some semblance of control. As we taxied onto the Epps ramp afterwards, Toots, the flight school mechanic was standing there. She was used to collecting my plane after each lesson to put the struts and gear back together again. Word had already reached the maintenance hanger that I was testing out one of Richard's 'prototype' arms. Rob had already opened the door to keep us cool, so as soon as I had shut her down, Toots wandered over.

"Well, Miss Tina, how did it go?"

" I think it went well – ask the boss."

Tootsie's eyebrows disappeared into her mass of glorious curly hair, as a stunned expression shot across her face.

"You tellin' me it worked?"

"Yep – it looks as if it worked. She's just done twelve reasonable landings with it over on runway niner," smiled Rob.

"Well...holy smoke, Tina, if you can do that girl – you can do anythang!" she laughed.

"You'd better hurry if you don't want to be late for your ground school lesson," Rob said. "I'll finish tying down the plane, you just get on in there."

I couldn't stop smiling, as I walked back into the school. The class had started. Jeff, my ground school instructor was busy explaining basic aerodynamics to a captivated audience. The other three members of the group were deep in concentration as I entered.

"So...who can tell me what makes an airplane turn?"

"Ailerons," came the reply.

"Well...you're not wrong...ailerons are the hinged surfaces fixed to the rear edge of aircraft wings to permit lateral control...but who can tell me which forces are at work...what has to happen to one wing to enable the aircraft to turn?"

Denis was sitting with his feet up on a desk, at the back of the class. His grin widened as I walked to my seat. I held my thumb up to him and grinned. Sandra, a private student, who had decided that, once her son was in college, she would do what she'd always wanted to do and learn to fly a plane, sat at the front of the class. Her face brightened up the room.

Ten minutes later, Jeff was saying:

"Well...that's a lot for you to be taking up all at once...we'll take a ten minute break there for you to catch your breath."

FORTY-THREE

The date was now August the seventeenth. In four days, it would be the third anniversary of my accident in Australia. I loathed this time, because try as I might, I couldn't help reliving all the events leading up to that dreadful afternoon. Everyone else in the group had flown solo now, so I knew I was next in line.

"Rob," I said, after one lesson, "how close am I to soloing?"

"You're very close," he replied, "all we need is another review of emergency landings, some consistency in your landings and of course some good weather."

I felt both excited and scared at his words.

"Why do you ask?"

"Well, it would mean a lot to me, if I could solo this Saturday."

"Why this Saturday?"

"Never mind why. I'll tell you after I've done it."

"Well I can't guarantee that you will be able to do it on Saturday. It all depends on how you are on that day...how the weather is...how busy the pattern is...so many things...but we'll see on the day, ay?"

He put his arm around my shoulder and gave me a squeeze.

"Tina, I'm so proud of the way you are working, you know."

I smiled, a thousand thoughts swimming around in my head.

* * *

My next flight with him was mediocre, nothing more. The one after that was appalling. It was as if I had forgotten everything I had ever learnt about flying. Totally crestfallen, I dragged everything in from the plane. The following day was the twenty-first of August. There was no hope at all of getting my 'tail-feathers cut' after my dismal performance.

Toots walked out onto the ramp. She looked over at me and smiled but I was too engrossed to see her.

"Hey, girl! You ignoring me or something?" she laughed.

"What? Oh, I'm so sorry Toots – I've just had the worst lesson you could imagine. I don't think I'll ever be able to solo, let alone tomorrow as I'd hoped."

"Oh, don't say that Miss Tina – it's always a good sign when you fluff things up before a first solo...makes you less complacent."

I looked up at her and grinned,

"You always know the right thing to say, Toots Mae."

"Oh...you be quiet now," she said awkwardly and walked off towards the *Arrow*.

"What's the weather going to do tomorrow?" I asked Kathy as I handed over the keys and checklist.

"Umm, let me see now," she said looking up to the board, "looks like there could be some mist and low cloud coming in from the east."

"Oh, great!" I said feeling relieved, and sad simultaneously.

I was petrified of doing it – but something inside me really wanted to do it on that particular day. It was almost as if it were my way of laughing in the face of adversity.

FORTY-FOUR

That night sleep evaded me. Each time I settled into a deep sleep, I kept seeing the wings of a great bird soaring to and fro through the sky. When I woke the next morning, I had a thick heavy head. I rubbed my eyes and remembered what day it was. I sat up in bed, shook away the melancholy, before it could get a grip on me. I slid out of bed and poked my head through the curtains. It was a dull and misty day. How disappointing. There was not going to be any flying done today. I got up and prepared for the day. Even if we couldn't fly, we still had to go in and study. The course was so intensive that no time could be wasted. We all piled into the cab feeling quite resentful that we couldn't spend the day studying in our rooms instead of hanging about in a dingy flight school.

"Good Morning everyone, how are we all today?"

"Fine, Thank you," we all mumbled back.

"No flying today, folks. Ceiling five hundred, haze and fog...visibility two and a half..." he said turning to Stuart, "Now, Stuart, what are the minimums we need for a VFR flight."

"Oh, no! He's on form today," Jane whispered over to me.

"Over to the ground school room, everyone...a test...I think...on the procedure you follow if your engine begins to run rough."

The morning dragged on and on and on. At break time, I wandered over to the desk.

"What's happening with the weather?"

"Pretty much the same old story...ceiling fifteen hundred scattered, five thousand overcast...visibility six...not a pretty day."

"But, Dave...that's not the same as this morning...that's heaps better."

"I'll tell you one thing it's not, though, Tina...," he said leaning on the counter and grinning, "...it's not good soloing weather...that's for sure...not with those ten knot winds blowing at ninety degrees to the runway."

"Oh...I suppose you're right," I said, returning to my ground school class.

"...full electrical failure, Tina...tell us what you would do if you experienced full electrical failure?"

And so, it dragged on until lunchtime. Then Bill Langtry wandered into the room.

"Anyone wish to join me for lunch at the *Cuban*?"

You could get one of the best sandwiches in Atlanta at the *Cuban*. Normally, I would have leapt at the chance, but today I felt slightly nauseous. I declined the offer and waved off the rest of the group.

'May as well do some studying,' I thought, and picked up my textbook. My medical certificate dropped out of it onto the desk. 'Oh, yes, I'd better put that with my log book.'

I had seen so many students, frantically searching every-where for their medical certificate just before they could solo. I wanted to be prepared if it ever happened.

I felt strange somehow. Not numb, as on the first two anniversaries of the accident, just flat, a little depressed. I would be glad when this day was over. It was so silent in the room; everyone in the whole building must have gone to lunch. I laid my head down on my arm, closed my eyes and sank into 'nothingness' again, just like that day when I was in the pool. I didn't feel like sleeping, I wasn't that tired. I just enjoyed emptying all the clutter out of my mind for just a few precious moments.

* * *

Several minutes later, the door banged open and a breathless voice brought me back to reality.

"There you are, Tina. I've been searching for you everywhere. Go get your arm on, cos, lady...*we're going flying."*

I struggled to put my brain back into gear, stammering,

"But what about the weather, Rob?"

"That wind has blown most of the cloud out of here...I'm not saying you can solo today, but at least we can have a lesson."

Now I knew why I hadn't felt like going out to lunch. Gathering together all my equipment, I scrambled along the corridor beside Rob.

"Wind's still a bit high, nine knots, and it's blowing ninety degrees across the runway...direct cross-wind...but that will be great practice for you."

I laughed. I felt strangely energised. Must have been that rest I'd just had in the ground schoolroom.

"Meet you in ten minutes at the plane," said Rob.

It struck me half way through my pre-flight, how meticulous I had become. Suddenly the idea of the flying a plane with a reliable engine carries far more impact, when you realise that at some stage you are going to be the only person there at the controls and you don't have an infallible instructor as a safety net. It was a shame that I wasn't going to be soloed today, but at least I was going up. I really did need to fly today, at least. I patted the spinner at the nose of Eight-Four-

221

Six-Six-Golf. I was starting to feel a real affinity with this plane.

Ten minutes later, Rob came bouncing towards the plane. He had that look in his eyes that I had only seen once before, when I had accompanied his family to his church. How I longed for the purity of mind and sense of purpose that he displayed. He jumped onto the wing and climbed in.

"Advise tower we're stayin' in the pattern," he said, "and don't forget what we do with the ailerons when taxiing. This wind is not to be ignored."

"Yes, Rob."

"Good, right let's go."

The wind was quite insistent in letting me know of its presence, as I taxied out to runway two-zero-right, but I preferred it like this. At least I knew what I was up against from the start. I couldn't be caught out.

As soon as we got onto downwind, I looked across at Rob and smiled. He was staring ahead, deep in concentration.

"Crab, Tina, crab. Come *on* now...turn the plane more towards the wind...you're *not* thinking where the wind is coming from. You *can't* ignore it...get some crab in *right* now or you'll get blown off course."

My first landing was good. I did a forward slip down onto the runway. Two or three landings later, I noticed Rob pick up the microphone and start talking.

"What are you doing?" I asked.

"Never mind what I'm doing, you keep your mind on the job."

I turned final and crabbed my way towards the runway, then just about fifty feet over the numbers, he suddenly bellowed, "Right! Do a go-round...do a go round now!"

"But, but...there's nothing wrong with my landing, I don't need to do a go round..."

"Don't argue with me, just do it and do it now..."

God! I thought this was going to be a pleasant lesson! I applied full power, and, flying parallel to the runway, built up enough speed to gradually release my flaps. As soon as I had everything under control, I called tower,

"Peachtree Tower, Eight-Four-Six-Six Golf doing go-round."

"Eight-four-six-six golf...fly right of runway. I will call your right turn," interjected the Tower.

"Flying right of runway...Six-Six-Golf"

"Watch your airspeed...nose on the horizon! Check your tracking. Good! That was good, Tina."

He then went silent. Nothing was said during my next four landings. I kept looking over to him for verification. If I asked him anything, he just shrugged saying,

"You're pilot in command, I'm just the passenger, how would I know?"

'He's behaving strangely today,' I thought.

We took off after my eighth landing and finally he broke the silence.

"Right...you've lost your engine, what are you going to do now?"

"Continue straight ahead and land on a suitable straight piece of land ahead."

"Such as...show me somewhere."

"That freeway over there," I replied pointing towards the Interstate 85.

"Why wouldn't you turn back to the airport?"

"Because I would lose too much height in the turn."

These answers were automatic now.

"Okay, ask for a full stop on your next call to tower and how about finding out what the wind is doing now – it may have changed, we've been flying for a while."

"Okay."

Coming into land I picked up the microphone

"Wind-check."

The reply came,

"Full cross wind at six knots."

"Oh, it's dropped."

I thought it felt as though it had.

As we taxied towards Epps ramp, Rob turned to me,

"You're ready, Tina. I'm gonna cut you loose."

"No, no I'm not. I can't do it on my own. I can't...I can't."

"You won't be on your own," he smiled, "*He'll* be sitting right here where I am, taking care of you!"

He thumped his hand down on the side of his seat.

"You were saved in Australia. You'll be protected again, today."

My heart went into overdrive. This guy was serious.

"Now don't park up, just taxi on down to the gate and I'll run in and get your log book and medical."

"I've already got it here."

He looked surprised.

"So, you *were* expecting it! Now just call tower as normal. I'm gonna run up to the tower now, so I'll be there at the end of the microphone, if you need me...but you know you won't. Now go for it, girl...and remember...you're not alone."

I went into automatic and found ATIS, noted the current local weather conditions, then called Peachtree Ground Control.

"Peachtree Ground this is Cherokee Eight-Four-Six-Six Golf at Epps gate ready to taxi VFR with information Juliet."

"Good afternoon Eight-Four-Six-Six Golf – taxi runway two zero right and contact tower."

They sounded very amiable. I wondered if Rob was already up there.

"Taxiing runway two-zero right – 66G," I said, sounding far calmer than I felt.

I looked to my right. The empty seat was certainly unnerving but, according to Rob, it wasn't empty. I wasn't alone.

"He'd better be there...," I said out loud, "because I'm going to need all the help I can get."

I pulled up at 20R and carried out my engine check, then contacted tower.

"Peachtree Tower this is Cherokee Eight-Four-Six-Six Golf holding runway 20R, ready for take-off."

"Cherokee Eight-Four-Six-Six Golf, Peachtree Tower, state direction of flight."

"Remaining in the pattern, 66G."

"Cherokee Eight-Four-Six-Six Golf cleared for take-off runway 20R. Good Luck!"

He was there! He was there! He was there!

I pulled onto the centre of the runway, nervously checked mixture setting, flaps and hand-brake for the sixty-seventh time and, with my yoke full over into the wind, I eased the throttle forward. As 'we' rolled out down the runway, I felt for the wind with the ailerons. Slowly we picked up more and more speed...

"Forty...forty, five...fifty...fifty five...rotation speed...ease back the yoke...no...not too sharply...keep it steady...check your tracking...'til in line with the runway...nose down...nose down on the horizon...seventy two...seventy two...keep it there...steady...more right rudder...verify you have full

throttle...coming up to five hundred feet...check all round...no traffic...right...turn upwind,"

Where was this voice coming from? I flipped my headphones – surely, Rob's not talking me through my solo? That's not allowed. I glanced over to the right seat. Empty.

Then all at once it dawned on me. Here I was flying a plane at five hundred feet and climbing and there was nobody to get me down. I had to do it myself. There had been too much to think about beforehand to realise the implications of what I was doing, until now and now, it was too late to change my mind. Either I landed the plane, or I flew around the sky until I ran out of fuel and crashed. I was doing this on my own, but *I didn't feel alone.* Half way along the downwind, I did my pre-landing check and pulled back the power to 1500 rpm.

"Oh, well, here goes...Peachtree Tower Cherokee Eight-Four-Six-Six Golf requests touch and go for runway 20R."

"Cherokee Eight-Four-Six-Six Golf cleared for touch and go 20R."

'Why hadn't I asked for a full-stop when I could?'

Lowering my pitch, I pulled back the power and lined myself up with the runway. The ground began to get nearer and nearer. Suddenly, I felt that same feeling I had felt exactly three years ago, as our car bounced, out of control, down the side of that hill. My throat constricted.

'This is just the same,' I thought, as the air began to whoosh past the windows.

'No it's not the same,' came that voice again, *'this is not the Outback of Australia and you are not out of control. Now fly, Tina, fly.'*

Taking hold of the controls, the plane gradually lost more and more altitude. When the time came, I flared, bringing the nose up gently. The plane floated down onto the runway, with the grace of a swan, to my utter astonishment. I released the flaps, flipped the ailerons full into the wind and applied full throttle. Then came the voice again, telling me exactly what to do. Was it in my head? I'll never know. Up, up I climbed. Slipping into the silvery beyond with the grace of a great, majestic bird.

As my beautiful white swan soared up into the sky, breaking out of its earthbound chains, I thought of *Jonathan*. Here I was flying, not only physically, but spiritually. This wasn't the end of my learning. It was the beginning. I was about to embark on the most thrilling journey of discovery and growth...the rest of my life.

"Come, now," I whispered to the silent power that had brought me thus far, *"I have finally allowed you to teach me to fly...let's go find my rainbow."*

* * *

It was a very different person that tied down the airplane and slid the keys across the counter to the dispatcher to hang up. I glanced up at the 'merit' board and my name was already up in big letters with the words 'congratulations on your first solo'. I couldn't stop grinning. I had done it. I had soloed an aircraft. But more than that, I knew for sure now that there was something out there. For the first in my life, I truly *believed*. It all suddenly became clear to me. I had not come here to learn to fly an aircraft. I had come to learn about having total faith in something outside my capacity of comprehension. Was this to be it, now? Was I now to return to my old life and continue, as I had been doing, before all these strange events had begun to take place? I did not think so, but could not see how it could be otherwise.

By now, I had struck up a firm friendship with the Chief Dispatcher, Kathleen Baxter. We shared many interests, including one of eating exotic food. This particular night, we had chosen to go to one of our favourite restaurants, an Ethiopian one down in Little Five Points. We always used these infrequent sorties to have lengthy discussions about matters affecting our lives at the time. Kathleen was expecting a baby and was bemoaning the fact that there didn't seem to be enough dispatchers working at the school. The larger she became with the child, the less work she could take on by herself. Trying to placate her, I looked at her and said,

"Well, I would do it myself, if I could."

"You would? I didn't think you'd be interested."

"Of course I'm interested, I'd love to be able to live here. There's not much chance though, because I haven't got a work permit or anything."

"I think that we could justify your being employed...you can be the liaison officer for the British disabled flying program. You have been through the program *and* you're disabled *and* you're British."

"Are you serious? You are serious, aren't you?"

"I am if you are."

We shook hands on it. The next part of my journey had been solved.

* * *

I waited three months before handing in my notice at the school. I wanted to be sure of getting the Temporary work permit before burning my bridges. I had an overwhelming feeling of guilt about leaving those children who had come to trust and depend on me. They could not believe that I was doing this. *I* could not believe that I was doing this to them. My mother just could not understand my desire to live and work in Atlanta. She would not discuss it at all, in the hope that, if undisturbed, the problem would go away. It did not. Like a big snowball rolling down the side of a mountain, the passing of time merely allowed it to gather momentum and force.

My colleagues were confused and bemused at the same time. They could not understand why I should want to give up a promising career to go and work in an office on the one hand, but I also detected more than a little envy at my shrugging off 'the system' in search of a new life.

"It just *feels* right," I would tell them, when they asked me what had made me do it.

And that was the only thing that I had to give me the courage to do what must have appeared to many, crazy and totally without logic. What they did not know was that there was a safety net for me. Margot and Pauline had convinced me that I had a watertight case against the people responsible for the upkeep of the roads. I had been told that there had been two fatal accidents along the same stretch of road that our accident had taken place. They had been instructed to tarmac it immediately and had not done so. I had a solicitor in Darwin working on suing these people. I did not know when, but I did know that there was a substantial amount of money coming my way. Had I not known this, I doubt if I would have been so quick to give up a good job in the teaching profession. It was just a matter of time, I kept telling myself.

I arrived in Atlanta with one suitcase and a pocket full of money from the sale of my car in England. By April Fool's

Day, I was standing behind the counter at Epps, trying to desperately remember the thousand and one things required of a flight school dispatcher. I had never expected it to be quite so demanding. Long stress-filled hours filled with little recompense. I thought I would never master the art of typing with one hand. Seventy thousand words later, I can say that I probably did! Arguments over English/American spellings, keeping on top of pilots' flying requirements, the weather, the phones etc., really did wake my brain and push it into top gear. One had to be so alert just to keep up. Aerobics for the brain, I called it later to a friend. Gradually I found that tasks, I thought I would never learn, became automatic. After a few months, I could allow myself the luxury of relaxing once in a while. I came to love and cherish the fleet of planes for which I was responsible. They became little friends, each one with it's own idiosyncrasies.

My favourite time was the early morning. I would open up the flight school at seven. Then I would walk across the Epps hanger to the front desk to collect any airplane keys left by night rental pilots. To get there, I would pass the élite princes of the upper echelons, poking their regal noses through the early morning mists that shrouded the airport each day. I would sensuously brush past the spinner of a *King Air*, trail my fingers over the fuel tank of a *Lear Jet* or simply wonder at the sheer majesty of a *Gulf Stream*. During our secret early morning rendezvous, these planes became kindred spirits sharing a love of the sky. I had a similar feeling towards the little fleet of flight school planes. It consisted mostly of *Piper Warriors*, a *Seminole* for multi-training, an *Arrow* for high-performance checkouts, and a cheeky little *Decathlon* for aerobatics training.

Every evening, I had to walk along the line, checking the tie-downs were secure, master switches were off, yolks were secured, doors locked and whether they needed fuel. If they did, I would turn the propeller to a vertical position so that the fuel truck would be able to see which planes needed fuel. I loved this part of the job. It felt as if I were tucking them into bed, as dusk crept over the horizon.

I was now renting a cosy little duplex (bungalow) within walking distance of the airport. This was important, because there was no way that I could be doing what I was doing *and* buy a car. I loved that little place, with its steep grassy drive and its winding creek running along the far end. I used to revel in being able to write home that I had filled the tiny front garden with flowers and had a creek full of crayfish in the back. I spent many an evening sitting on the back step, watching the fireflies dance amongst the Georgia Pines, being serenaded by the crickets and the bullfrogs. It was all so different – so very different to life back in England.

One day, my delightful little picture was shattered. I was lounging on the couch with the screen door closed, but the main door open. Suddenly I looked through the screen door to see a man in his early twenties, dressed in what appeared to be combat gear, brandishing a shotgun. I sat bolt upright as he shouted through the screen door, in a real twangy Georgian accent,

"Ma'am...would y'all mind if I shoot that Copperhead snake living in y'alls creek...my dawg swims in there and I'm feared for his safety."

"N-no," I spluttered, eyes like saucers, "You go ahead."

I had no idea what a Copperhead was, nor that it was a highly poisonous snake. I was more worried about the young man and his gun. I never went frolicking barefoot along the edge of the creek from that day forth.

At first, I purchased two cheap beds. Then I rented everything else for a few dollars a week. That way, I figured that I could gradually replace the rented furniture with my own as and when I could afford it. The strange thing was that I never did have to afford it. Things began to 'appear' – things that I needed.

I befriended two ladies from the neighbourhood. One, Sarah, turned up on my doorstep one night during a particularly ferocious storm. She burst into my life wearing canary-yellow galoshes and southwester. I knew she was a 'Brit' before she uttered a word. She was a very *British* 'Brit'. Her elegance, kindness and dry-witted humour were a great comfort to me in those early days away from the 'mother country'. Sarah would always turn up with a couple of forks in her pocket, or a bowl of pansies, just as my spirits began to wane. Her friend, Stori, mother of eight, with barely two cents to rub together, would often send down a bowl of something she had just made.

These two women were masters in the art of finding the most exquisite items at yard sales or on the side of the road. They would go on long reconnaissance walks around the neighbourhood to see what had been discarded. This was perfectly normal practice. Everyone did it. It was a way of recycling furniture. Often the phone would ring at my office and there would be an excited voice at the other end saying, "Tina, there's a lovely dresser on the street at Carlton road...if you want it, say now so that we can get it to your house before it rains..."

This was how I replaced much of the rented furniture in my house. A pattern started to emerge. I would wish for something, or happen to mention it to someone and, lo and behold, there it would be sitting on my doorstep the next day.

By that time Jane, one of my fellow scholarship winners, was lodging with me. Even she used to turn up with all sorts of amazing kitchen gadgets. We had microwaves, televisions, coffee makers, mixers – everything you could wish for. One day she thrust a book in my hand. It was a copy of *'Bridge Across Forever'*.

"I know you like that author," she had said with a wry grin on her face.

I had never known anything quite like this before. I was able to furnish the whole house for just a few dollars. It was a miracle and I thanked God every day for my good fortune. I had needed it and how I loved my little house and all its contents.

Then the shoulder joint of my one remaining arm seized up. I let it go on until it was no longer possible to dress or wash properly because of the pain. I had no health insurance at the time and hoped that it would go away. It did not.

One night, I was attending my instrument flying ground school, when I noticed that, across the room, a friend was watching me struggle into my jacket. He strode over and asked me why I was having such a problem dressing. I told him there was something wrong with my shoulder. He wanted to see it. It turned out that he was an orthopaedic surgeon specializing in arthroscopic surgery. This was precisely what I needed. He told me to be at his office the very next day.

* * *

I was examined, operated on and out of hospital within a few weeks. I had a shoulder socket that was almost like new – and he did not charge me for his service, nor did he once make me feel in any way beholden to him.

On leaving hospital, I did have a slight problem with sleeping. I could not put any pressure on the shoulder, so every time I twisted and turned on the hard mattress, I would awake in excruciating pain.

'If only I had a soft place to sleep', I thought to myself.

The next day a flight instructor, from a neighbouring school, wandered into my office.

"Tina, D'you know anyone who wants a water bed. I'm moving and can't take it with me. I don't want anything for it and I will deliver it...just want it off my hands."

"I know just the person," I replied.

It had happened again.

* * *

For the past year, I had been teaching Latin to Stori's eldest son, Sam. They had wanted to recompense me in some way, but that was not what I wanted. I enjoyed the lessons and felt this was my way of repaying them for all they did for me. Despite this, on several occasions, I would discover a crumpled envelope pushed under my door with some dollars in it. I did not know what to do. I certainly did not want to be paid, but I did want our lessons to continue. Finally, a few days before Christmas, the problem was solved. Stori rushed into my house, breathless and bursting with excitement.

"Tina, oh Tina you're never going to believe what has happened."

"What?" I replied, guessing from her exuberance, that it was not bad news.

"Someone from our church has given us an old car...we don't need it, but we know you do. It may only last for three weeks or so, but that will be better than three weeks of cab fares...won't it?"

I thought I was dreaming. The one thing that I had not been able to afford, and desperately needed, was a car, but that had been out of the question. I started to cry with joy.

"I cannot believe it...are you sure? Oh, Stori, this is the best Christmas present that I ever had," I took her by the hand and shook it about, "this is the most amazing thing that has happened to me."

"Remember, Tina, it is just an old car...it may not last long...wait until you see it...it's old and worn."

"I don't care, I love it already."

That 1977 *Dodge Aspen* didn't last me three weeks. It lasted three years (with a little help from the flight school mechanics and Stori's husband, Joe). I cherished it. Neither the rusty chasms in the wings, the 'air-conditioning' holes in the roof, nor the atmospheric, billowing red velvet material that had come unstuck from the inside of the roof, could detract from the beauty of this fine car. The shining chrome-fronted machine with the V-8 engine carried me around Atlanta as smoothly as if I were floating on water.

The only time it broke down was right at the top of my drive. Firstly, it had got me home safe, then spluttered and died right in front of the house. When I left, it was given to another person who was hurting for money. One year later, I returned to Atlanta and tried to buy it back for a thousand dollars. The owner refused. I guess he must have loved it as much as I did.

My life in Atlanta was about as happy as I had been any-where. I adored my little home. I had a wonderful group of friends. My job was exciting and demanding. I was flying and I had the '*Shadow Car*', as it had been christened by one of my friends. I was still quite heavily in debt to the hospital where I'd had my arthroscopic surgery, as well as the IRS (after they decided, after a whole year working in the States and not paying tax, that they had made a mistake and I was liable for payment in full)! I was constantly running to the bank with ten-dollar bills to stop a check from bouncing. Still, that would be all paid in a few months and I would be able to breathe again. This, I kept reassuring myself, was God's way of teaching me the real value of money before I get my compensation.

* * *

Happy times in Atlanta, Georgia

Then, one stifling morning in June, the final blow came. I awoke one morning with a dull, persistent ache in my side. Within a couple of hours at work, I was crumpling in a heap on the floor in agony.

"Appendix...that's what I reckon...appendix," said Bill in a matter of fact way.

"I have no appendix!" I replied.

"I'm taking her to Doctor Maclean right now...Bill, you take the desk," shouted Sandra as she led me to her car outside.

I tried to sit up in the car but it was impossible. I flipped the front seat as far back as it would go and lay on it.

"It could be a number of things...but, whatever it is, it is acute. She needs to be hospitalised. I'm sending her to Ringford Hospital...to Doctor Christine Ekert. Here are her forms Sandra...do you know where the Peachtree entrance is?"

"Of course I do...come on, Teen."

It seemed just seconds later that the doctor was looking down at me on the stretcher and saying,

"The tests show that there is some kind of cyst on your left ovary. We're going to have to operate...not a big operation...laser surgery...but it must be carried out immediately."

"I cannot afford an operation right now," I said helplessly.

"You cannot afford *not* to have surgery right now, Christina."

There was nothing I could do. The surgery was done and, before I knew it, I was home – alone. I felt desolate as I lay in my water bed with my beloved cat 'Sid' lying beside me on the pillow licking my forehead. By my calculation, I would have to find at least $2,000 of the hospital bill. I simply did not have it. I called two friends, cap in hand, shamefully asking them to loan me the money. To my horror, they were in the same position as me and felt almost as dreadful having to say no as I had for asking. These were dark days, indeed. My blood pressure finally soared through the roof and I was told to go home and lie down until the medication could get it under control. I will remember that awful feeling in the pit of one's stomach one experiences under these circumstances, for as long as I live. The lesson I was learning here could be taught to me no other way. There is a world of difference between knowing things like this happen and actually experiencing them at first hand. Finally, in a fit of desperation, I wrote to my solicitor in Australia, who was handling my claim. I told him to settle the claim right now and accept whatever we were offered, because I needed the money right now. Thankfully, he refused, deciding to make me an interest-free loan to be reimbursed upon the settlement of the claim. When *would* the claim be settled? It had been seven years now. He would not commit himself.

Then, at long last, a letter arrived from Australia. We were going to court. He wanted me to get out there and spend a month having all my final assessments and reports done in Australia before the court hearing. Then, he stressed, if it went to appeal, I could be out there for three months or more.

"Three months!" I said, "I can't pay my rent for three months without any income, and they're not going to keep my job open for three months, either!"

"I know," he replied.

So, I was forced to resign - thus losing my US. Temporary Work Permit *and* breaking up my sweet little 'yard-sale palace' *and* giving away my beloved cat. Having sold everything I owned in my own yard-sale, I left for England, my very uncertain future hanging in the balance. No job. No home. Everything I owned pushed into two suitcases. I felt an absolute failure. What if I lost the case? There was always a chance that might happen.

I had very mixed feelings about being home. It was as though I had failed to make it in some way. The past few years had been tough, but happy ones. I now found myself in a kind of limbo, not having any idea of how the future would unfold. I only had the present to hold on to. My first task was to find a way of getting to Australia as cheaply as possible. My Mother offered to loan me the money. I found, what seemed, a great deal and pulled out my suitcase once again. My solicitor was on the phone every other day now with varying news about the case. Then, one morning, as I walked through the front door, my mother almost knocked me down as she said,

"Where have you been? Your solicitor has called three times trying to reach you. He said it was vital he spoke to you immediately...go on, call him now...he's waiting."

"What did he want, did he say?"

"No. He would only speak to you."

I dialled the number and my call was put through to his office.

"Daniel, it's Tina. What's wrong?"

"Nothing's wrong...I believe we have finally frightened them into making an out of court settlement...they've come up with an offer...remember this is their first offer and we don't have to accept anything...we could possibly make double this in court...but there again, there's always the chance we might be offered considerably less..."

I had always had a figure in my mind that was what I felt would be a fair compensation. The offer was over twice that amount. If I did settle out of court, there would be no court appearance, travel or stress. For seven years, I had wanted to close the book on this particular part of my life, but this on going litigation meant that I forever had to dredge through old memories. I'd had enough. It was time for closure.

"Accept the offer," I said, with conviction.

"But, Christina, think about this carefully. There's a lot at stake here..."

"Accept the offer," I said once more.

It was time to move on. My life had been on hold for the past seven years. Enough was enough.

"Okay, Christina. It is your decision. I will inform them of your wishes immediately."

"Thanks, Daniel. I'll talk to you soon."

On replacing the receiver, relief flooded over me. It was finally over. I stared at the phone. It was over, but at what cost? One couldn't put a figure on life itself. I had lost part of my life, my home, my job and, more importantly, my work visa for the States. And the irony of it all was that I need not have done.

* * *

A few weeks later, Daniel informed me that he had just wired the money to England and it should be in my account as soon as it had been cleared by all the relevant authorities – a couple of weeks at the most.

When ten days had gone by, I began calling the bank.

"Is it here yet?" I would inquire of the Personal Banker

"No, not yet, Tina."

Every day I phoned the bank or went in.

"Is it h.."

"No, Tina, not yet. I'll call you as soon as it arrives."

I kept up this vigil day after day. Where was it? Had somebody intercepted it and run off with it all? I was starting to worry.

Then, one morning, I decided to call a friend and invite her to meet me down town to do some shopping and have a coffee. We'd just done all the shopping, and were heading full speed towards the Coffee Shop, when I realised that, for the first time in two weeks, I had passed the bank without going in.

"You're certainly taking my mind off things...I've just passed the bank and not thought about going in...ha, ha...they must be sick of me badgering them."

We took a few more steps...then, stopping in my tracks, I did an about turn.

"Oh, what the hell...as long as I'm here I may as well pop in...d'you mind?"

"No, not at all."

I breezed in through the doors, looked over at Martin and, before I'd had a chance to mouth the words, he said, "Yes."

"What d'you mean...'yes'?"

"I mean it's here."

I went white as a sheet and started to tremble.

"Are you sure...I mean...is it really?"

He was as pleased as I was.

"Yes, yes, yes! Now come and sit down and I'll tell you how much it converted to in pounds sterling."

It still hadn't really sunk in as I stood up, grabbed my friend by the hand, walked out of the bank, did a 'U-turn' into the jewellers and pointed to an exquisite three carat diamond ring in the window.

"I'd like to buy that one, please."

Five minutes later, we were leaving the shop, the dazzling ring sitting very well on my finger. Next stop was the pub. Cocktails all round. My friend was as caught up in all the excitement as I. Her face glowed, as she lent over to me and said, "When you called and asked me to come shopping with you, I wasn't expecting *this!*"

We both roared with laughter, the mixture of the excitement and alcohol making us both quite heady.

* * *

After the dust had taken time to settle, I decided to go to church. I sometimes feel rather like a hermit crab in church, because I simply use the building as a means of communing with God, or that Universal Power that guides us all. To me, what we call the Power, or how we do it, is irrelevant. This particular day, I chose a Catholic Church. It was a Eucharist service. I sat unobtrusively, trying to fix my mind on getting 'tuned in'. I visualised myself standing with my arms raised upward, saying,

"Okay, God. You have brought me this far. Now what? I have no home, no job, but I do have some money. Why have I been freed up like this? What am I to do next? Where am I to go?"

Even before I had finished formulating these questions, I had the answer. One word: *Patience* was slipped through the letterbox of my mind. I left the church feeling rather like a child who had been rebuked. But the more I thought about it, the more I began to see the wisdom of this message. I was still in poor health and, to be honest, was useless to anyone until I had regained that. My blood-pressure was still unstable. I was over-weight and totally out of condition. Suddenly, I remembered a conversation I'd had with Sandra, while still working at the Flight School.

"As soon as you get your money, Teen, I'll tell you what you want to do...book straight into that Spa in Florida...in fact," she grabbed the phone and slid her glasses onto the end of her nose, "I'm gonna get them to send you a brochure right now," she exclaimed, licking her index finger and proceeding to flip through the pages of the phone book.

I knew that I had tucked that brochure into my case before leaving Atlanta. As soon as I arrived home, I dashed upstairs and started shuffling through the files of printed matter that I had dragged home. The brochure was still there. On opening it, I discovered that it was a modern version of the original spa of that name located in Tuscany, Italy. I read on.

"...*this Spa (lat. Salve Per Aqua, meaning 'health through water') legend has it, was formed as a direct result of Saturn, God of War, returning from battle and deciding that he would never fight another. He threw his spear up in to the air and where it landed, a spring sprang forth, sending health-giving waters high in to the air. The area where the spring appeared was named Saturnia, after the God. People have been bathing in the waters since before Roman times...*"

A month later, I found myself sitting in a plush taxi, winding its way along the narrow roads of the Tuscan countryside.

"Look, here!" the driver would command, pointing to a tiny white church, perched on the brow of some gentle hill, over to our left, "Is Toscana...you like?"

It was dusk. The little rolling hills all around seemed to be bathed in a warm, peach coloured glow. Here and there, the flow of the landscape was interrupted by a row of cypress trees or the regimented rows of an olive grove. The air seemed velvety and smelt of freshly cut hay. I took a deep breath, drinking in the atmosphere, exhaled and replied,

"Yes, Enrico, I really like."

My response pleased him. It was as if the compliment was for him, personally.

"Thank you," he said, smiling bashfully and puffing out his chest, like a peacock. We drove on, a pleasant silence between us. This place didn't need words.

Suddenly, I reached down and wrenched off my false arm and threw it in the back of the taxi.

"Don't think I'll be needing this here," I said to an astonished Enrico.

"No, la senora will have no need for that," he smiled a knowing smile.

The famous spa water assaulted the senses as we made the final turn down the driveway of the hotel. Rotten eggs! The sulphur in the waters, which bubbled up from the bed of an old volcano at eight hundred thousand gallons an hour, took some getting used to.

"So...Christina, you have come here to let the waters heal your high blood-pressure, yes? You did not know that people have been coming here to treat blood-pressure problems since Roman times...you didn't know? What made you choose Saturnia, then? You say it *felt right*...I see."

The chic *doctoressa* was carrying out her preliminary examination before letting me embark on the slimming program offered there. So far, I hadn't laid eyes on a single fat person. I left the office and, to my delight, there sat a tall, elegant black woman with at least as much weight to shed as I. Quite suddenly, her face broke into a wide smile and her large brown eyes shone joyously, as she gently lowered her head in acknowledgement of me. We instantly became friends, fellow sufferers together. She was from the Sudan and was a Moslem. I was a Christian from England. We could not have come from backgrounds that were more different if we tried.

And yet, we felt like we were sisters. We laughed constantly, as we rambled through the Tuscan hills at the crack of dawn each day, stealing fruit from the bountiful trees and bushes that hung tantalizingly along our way. The Doctoressa cried to the heavens in frustration, when our weight did not drop as rapidly as it should have been doing.

"I don't understand it. You are eating the food I set...you are going on long walks everyday...you are doing the daily gym classes...and yet you lose just one pound this week...?"

We would both shrug our shoulders and look hurt.

"Der scales are wrong!" Nawa would declare, winking at me and knowing all the time that the problem was that we always returned from our walks with bellies full of fresh figs, blackberries and whatever else we could lay our hands on.

The Spa Manageress was a deceptively frail-looking woman in her forties, with the strength of character that resembled a freight train hurtling down a mountain at a hundred miles an hour. We, too, having a common language, found an instant rapport with each other. She hailed from America.

"Have you met him yet?" She hissed at me one day.

"Met who?"

"The Ambassador."

"What Ambassador?"

"Nawa's husband."

"What? She told me that her husband was bringing the children today and she wanted me to meet him...but I didn't know he was an Ambassador."

I immediately became nervous and shifted uneasily in my seat. Then there was a commotion at the restaurant door and in marched Nawa, draped in an opulent creation of silk and gold, followed by seven children and a stylishly dressed gentleman. I shrank down in my seat. Perhaps they would not notice me in this corner. They didn't at first, and then, as I was finishing my meal, one of the children ran across to my table saying, "My mother wants you to join her, come...come," he said, beckoning me.

I walked over to their table and he rose from his chair and turned to me, holding out his hand. He was a handsome with an athletic physique.

"This is Christina," Nawa said.

He took my hand and shook it gently saying, "It is a pleasure to meet you...Nawa talks about you all the time."

I was tongue tied and felt foolish.

"She misses you," I blurted out.

"Not as much as I miss her."

We laughed and spent the rest of the afternoon together.

* * *

I was to learn a great deal from Nawa. We would sit and have long discussions about religion and life and love. Each weekend she would leave the spa. A bodyguard would arrive in an enormous white *Mercedes* and whisk her off to their ambassadorial residence in Rome. They kept inviting me, but I felt it would be an intrusion.

Finally, they insisted. I, too, climbed into the big white *Mercedes* and sped away to Rome and all the culinary delights awaiting us there. On nearing Rome, some time later, the ambassador pulled out his phone and dialled a number. "Hello...Hassler Hotel...this is Ambassador Mahmoud...fine thank you...I come to eat tonight...three...your best table... thank you."

I hardly dare hope that the reservation was for us. I had

already heard about the Hassler...it was one of the finest places to dine in Rome.

The residence was like something out of the Palace of Versailles - sumptuously decorated in golds and whites. After I had been shown my room, I freshened up by taking a shower in the en suite bathroom. I was just about to climb out of the shower when I saw the gardener outside the bathroom window pruning the roses. He seemed to be staring right at me. I curled up with embarrassment, grabbed a towel, and rushed back into the bedroom and slipped into a nice dress, still not knowing if we were dining out.

This happened several more times before I noticed that the windows were one way ones. You could see out but nobody could see in.

When I joined Nawa back in the sitting room, she told me we were going to dine in Rome. I was thrilled. We sat chattering and laughing, when the ambassador came into the room. He seemed flustered.

"Come, come. We leave now, or not at all."

We jumped to attention and followed him out to the car. After a few minutes, Nawa began speaking in Arabic to her husband, then turned to me saying, "Christina, tell my husband about how you lost the use of your arm before you lost the arm."

Feeling as if I were on show, I recounted the tale about how I had not been able to use my left hand for the two months preceding the accident. At the end of it, he took a deep breath and then asked me why I thought it had happened like this.

"I can only think that I was somehow being prepared for what was to come," I answered.

"No, no..." the ambassador snapped, "Don't you see? It is clear to me that you had sickness in your arm and Allah removed the sickness to save your life."

I was stunned. I had never considered it from that angle before. Nobody could find a single reason for the disabling pain in the left wrist, but they were only looking for a problem in the bones. The God in my explanation now appeared to be callous and manipulative. This new explanation demonstrated a powerful and caring God.

The ambassador continued, "Allah loves you. That is why he wants you to live."

I was now lost in my thoughts, 'So...this means that the accident was not a punishment. It was a life-saving act.'

The arm was long gone now and who knows where it went, so there was no way of proving that this was so. Had there been some divine intervention? If so, why? What lay ahead?

He pulled up beside a sign that said 'No Parking' and laughed, "I have Government plates...I am allowed to park anywhere."

The Hassler positively exuded opulence. Crimson carpets and mahogany panelled walls hung with ancient masterpieces. As soon as the tiny antiquated elevator sounded its arrival at the roof top restaurant, the doors were pulled opened and a group of waiters almost fell over each other to lead us to the best table in the room. As we were seated, I glanced out of the windows in awe of the view it offered. From here, one could see Rome at its best. The sun was setting, providing a glowing backdrop of peach and orange. I was speechless.

"*Now* you see why I wanted to get you here as soon as possible. If we had arrived just two minutes later, we would have missed this," he said, waving his hand, triumphantly towards the window.

I sat there trying to convince myself that all this was not a · dream. At that moment, the very air that I breathed seemed to buzz with excitement and anticipation. This was a charmed life that I was leading. It appeared that the more I surrendered my life to fate and followed my intuition, the more fascinating it became.

* * *

The manageress phoned as soon as I opened the door to my hotel room back at the spa.

"Well...how was it? Come down and join me for a *Bellini* cocktail. I want to hear everything. Oh, and the books that I want you to read have arrived. I had them shipped from New York."

"Books?"

"Oh, just some light reading I have for you."

"I'll be right down, Eve."

The books turned out to be the first of many spiritual and metaphysical volumes that she would pass my way. I did not know why she did this, nor by now did I care. I devoured these books with a voracious appetite. It almost felt as if this whole experience was some kind of balm being poured onto my wounds. I was writing every day now and suddenly found that I could paint. My soul was being well and truly nourished. I kept waking up and thinking, 'What have I done to deserve all this.'

Before I knew it, my three months in paradise were over. Panic started to set in. I did not want to leave this place, but I knew that I must. I had lost a considerable amount of weight; my blood pressure was under control. I examined my face in the mirror. My face shone with health and my eyes...something had changed about my eyes, but I could not say what, exactly.

On our last night at the spa, Nawa and I donned our full-length evening dresses and finery, almost floating into the spa lounge. Umberto, the barman glanced over at us as we entered the room. He looked down and then, realising that it was us, shot us a wide grin as he rushed to greet us from behind his bar.

He paused before us, his appreciative eyes travelled over us. Sighing deeply, he clasped his hands together whispering, *"Elegantissime...elegantissime!"*

Suddenly it was all worth the effort. We both felt and looked a million dollars. It was time to move on.

* * *

On returning to England, I could not settle and, before long felt myself being pulled towards the States once more. I decided to return to Atlanta, but knew immediately that this was not where I ought to be. It seemed as if the longer I remained in a place that did not feel right, the more drained my spirit became. The one thing I was frightened of was undoing the work that I had done at the spa. I decided to take Eve up on her offer of letting me stay at her luxury villa on the Caribbean Island of Saint Marten. But before leaving, I called a travel agent and left instructions to book me onto the *Golden D'Or Spa* for a few weeks, upon my return.

* * *

The villa was incredible, with it's breathtaking view of the sea and Japanese inspired swimming pool, but I still did not feel that this was the right place for me.

On returning to Atlanta, I called the travel agent to check that my spa stay had been confirmed. "Oh, Christina, hi..." she had said, "The *Golden D'Or* could not accommodate you for the time you requested...so I went ahead and booked you into another spa...it's called *Green Valley*...you'll love it...I just know you will!"

I couldn't believe I was hearing this. "You mean you've gone ahead and booked me into a spa I've never heard of, without consulting me?"

"You'll love it," she replied. "Just trust me on this one, Christina, I know that you will love it."

Something in her manner made me bite my tongue and simply accept this unexpected turn of events.

"You leave on Monday...flying first to Las Vegas, then onto St. George in Utah in a small plane."

This was bizarre. I had no idea where Utah was. Anyway, despite not a small amount of trepidation, I packed my bag and embarked upon my adventure to St. George, Utah. The journey seemed endless and more than once, I questioned the logic of what I was doing. Finally, late into the evening, my cab rolled to a stop outside *Green Valley*. I clambered out impatiently, hot, dusty and frazzled around the edges. All I wanted to do was climb into the shower then sink into bed.

As soon as I set foot in the door, it was as if I had entered a different world. Before I could introduce myself, my cases were whisked away from me. Then a smiling girl, dressed in a luminescent white chiffon dress, seemed to 'float' towards me.

"Welcome to *Green Valley*, Christina," she whispered in my ear, leading me down a long corridor.

Aromatic oils and burning candles scented the air, while ethereal sounding music emanated from every corner. We entered a room filled with over-stuffed couches, crocheted drapes and plants tumbling from everywhere there was a space to put them. The girl pulled out a chair and invited me to sit down.

"I am going to give you a hand massage now. Just sit there and unwind while I fetch a bowl of water."

I was left alone in the room. The soft music played on. I heard the sound of running water and glanced over towards it. Standing in the centre the room was a fountain, surrounded by a magnificent display of crimson roses and a large red bowl filled with pale pink water. Rose petals floated on it's surface. The girl returned, smiling again. She took my hand, bathed it in the sweet smelling water and patted it dry, then proceeded to massage it gently with oil. She then offered me a glass goblet, filled with the pale pink drink and rose petals.

"How do you feel?" she whispered.

"Much better now, thanks." I replied in equally hushed tones.

"Good. Now, shall I show you to your villa?" she asked.

"Yes, that would be great, thanks. Where is everyone?"

There wasn't a soul to be seen.

" Oh...they're all in bed."

It was eight-thirty. When I got to my villa, I found the table set for one and a trout dinner in the fridge. I ate it, showered and went to bed.

I rose with the birds the following day. We were to be climbing in the canyons of Zion National Park. I had been told that everyone gathered in the dining room before leaving. Nervously, I pushed open the glass door, got a bowl of raison oatmeal and sat at the end of a long table. Everyone seemed to know each other already. I felt a little awkward and so pretended to be engrossed in reading the schedule for the day.

"Hi...do you mind if we join you for breakfast?" said a smiling face.

"No, not at all. Please do," I replied, grateful for some company.

"I'm Joan and this is my daughter, Kendra," as her hands reached up, gathered up her splendid long tresses and swept them down her back.

"My name is Christina, nice to meet you."

"Oh, Kendra ...she's English! We knew we would like you as soon as you walked through the door."

In no time at all, we fell into a congenial banter, as if we had been friends for years. Joan and Kendra came from a town, just north of San Francisco, called Berkeley. Their honesty and lack of inhibitions made them instantly appealing. Joan had been a hippie in Berkeley during the student uprisings of the sixties, although, with her long hair, youthful complexion and jeans, I found it hard to believe. Kendra was a beauty, but was totally unaware of this. She possessed the figure, looks and elegance equal to any model strutting the catwalk in Milan, but would never believe it if you told her. They both seemed to have the ability to make whoever they met feel as though they were worth a million dollars. Most of them probably were.

Soon it was time to clamber into the mini-buses and head off to Zion. Just as we were settling into our seats, a third lady appeared, sat down next to Joan and tried to get her breath back.

"Oh...good! We thought you weren't coming," exclaimed Joan.

"Well, I nearly didn't. Then I remembered it was Zion today. I didn't want to miss that."

"Guess what, Leslie. We have found a beautiful new friend. Leslie, meet Christina, our new English friend."
Feeling foolish, I lent forward and greeted Leslie.

* * *

The scenery along the way was more and more spectacular as each canyon seemed to dwarf the one before. Soaring red and orange edifices as high as our craning necks would allow us to see. Nobody could speak. We gazed out of the window in awe-struck silence.

On top of the world – climbing the canyons of Utah

From left to right: Leslie Parrish-Bach, Climb Guide, Joan, Me, Kendra, Director of Entertainment Tonight

An hour later, the mini-bus pulled to a stop beside some rapids. We climbed out, made a pit-stop at the bathroom and started to make our way up to a place called 'Angel's Landing'. Kendra joined the fast walkers, who promptly zoomed off into the distance, leaving behind them a cloud of dust. The slowest walkers made for the 'Emerald Pools'. Our little group decided that they wanted something more taxing than 'Emerald Pools', so we optimistically opted for a slower climb to 'Angel's Landing'.

We meandered along, marvelling at the scenery and silently experiencing the spiritual power it offered. We listened to the wind rustling the leaves, marvelled at the tenacity of the tiny birds that swooped along the path and sometimes we just stopped, drinking in the peaceful atmosphere. In time, even our group segmented into smaller groups. Joan, Leslie and I fell into such a group. The way ahead began to get extremely strenuous. We started to chat amongst ourselves to take our mind off things. Leslie began to ask about my arm. The part about the aborigines seemed to fascinate her. Suddenly she stopped in her tracks, her eyes fixed on a gold locket I was wearing around my neck.

"Christina...can I ask you a question?" she said.

"Of course," I replied, intrigued at what was going to come next.

"Why do you have pilot's wings engraved onto your locket?"

I was taken aback and stated the obvious,

"Because I'm a pilot."

Not satisfied with my response, she went on,

"But, how can you possibly do soft-field landings with one-arm?"

I was surprised that she had asked this, since only another

pilot would realise the problems involved.

"How come you know so much about flying?" I grinned, realising that I was now in the presence of a fellow pilot.

"Well...I'm married to one of the most famous pilots in the world...I guess."

"Oh, really. Who's that then? I may have heard of him," I ventured.

Almost like in a dream, she casually replied,

"His name is Richard Bach."

Serendipity smacked me between the eyes with such force I almost fell off the side of the ledge upon which I was balanced. I froze in my tracks. My face prickled and burned, with fear of how this had happened – and joy that it had. I felt as if this whole thing had been somehow divinely choreographed. Leslie, too, had decided to go to the spa at the very last minute. I could hardly breathe. I was hearing drumming in my ears. Everything was starting to make sense now. Nobody could have had more impact upon the direction of my life than Jonathan's earth mother. He must have led me here. How could this be an accident?

I tuned back in to Leslie once again.

"Christina..." she was saying, "I really do think that you ought to get your story written down before you start to forget... No, you don't need a ghostwriter... That doesn't matter, I'll teach you to word process. If we want to get this done, we can't afford the luxury of negative thought. Accidents don't just happen, Christina. You have been given a second chance. Now, seize it and run. Life, no matter how short or long, is for living. Now, go live it!"

To be continued...